Also by Gregory Boyle

Tattoos on the Heart

Barking
to the
Choir

The Power of
Radical Kinship

Gregory Boyle

Simon & Schuster Paperbacks
New York London Toronto Sydney New Delhi

Simon & Schuster Paperbacks
An Imprint of Simon & Schuster, Inc.
1230 Avenue of the Americas
New York, NY 10020

First Simon & Schuster trade paperback edition September 2018

SIMON & SCHUSTER PAPERBACKS and colophon are registered
trademarks of Simon & Schuster, Inc.

For information about special discounts for bulk purchases, please contact
Simon & Schuster Special Sales at 1-866-506-1949
or business@simonandschuster.com.

The Simon & Schuster Speakers Bureau can bring authors to your live event. For
more information or to book an event contact the Simon & Schuster Speakers
Bureau at 1-866-248-3049 or visit our website at www.simonspeakers.com.

Interior design by Lewelin Polanco

Manufactured in the United States of America

9 10

Library of Congress Cataloging-in-Publication Data

Names: Boyle, Greg, author.
Title: Barking to the choir : the power of radical kinship / Gregory Boyle.
Description: New York : Simon & Schuster, 2017.
Identifiers: LCCN 2017035498| ISBN 9781476726151 (hardcover) | ISBN
9781476726168 (trade pbk.)
Subjects: LCSH: Church work with juvenile delinquents—California—
East Los Angeles. | Christian life—Anecdotes. | Boyle, Greg.
Classification: LCC BV4464.5 .B69 2017 | DDC 277.94/94083—dc23 LC
record available at https://lccn.loc.gov/2017035498

ISBN 978-1-4767-2615-1
ISBN 978-1-4767-2616-8 (pbk.)
ISBN 978-1-4767-2617-5 (ebook)

For Mike Hennigan
Marge Sauer

and

Kathleen Conway Boyle

CONTENTS

INTRODUCTION

S tart with a title.

It's a terrible way to write a book.

So I'm in my office at Homeboy Industries talking with Ramón, a gang member who works in our bakery. Lately, he has been veering into the lane of oncoming traffic. He's late for work, sometimes missing it entirely, and his supervisors tell me he is in need of an emergency "attitude-ectomy." I'm running it down to him, giving him *"kletcha"*—schooling him, grabbing hold of the steering wheel to correct his course. He waves me off and says, self-assuredly, "Don't sweat it, bald-headed . . . You're barking to the choir."

Note to self: title of my next book.

I immediately liked, of course, the combo-burger nature of his phraseology. The marriage of "barking up the wrong tree" to "preaching to the choir." It works. It calls for a rethinking of our status quo, no longer satisfied with the way the world is lulled into operating and yearning for a new vision. It is on the lookout for ways to confound and deconstruct.

What gets translated in Scripture from the Greek *metanoia* as "repent" means "to go beyond the mind we have." And the "barking" is directed at the "Choir"—those folks who "repent" and truly long for a different construct, a radically altered way of proceeding and who seek "a better God than the one we have." The gospel can expose the game in which "the Choir" can find itself often complacently stuck. The game that keeps us from the kinship for which we long—the endless judging, competing, comparing, and terror that prevents us from turning the corner and bumping into that "something new." That "something" is the entering of the kinship of God . . . here and now, no longer satisfied with the "pie in the sky when we die."

The Choir is everyone who longs and aches to widen their "loving look" at what's right in front of them. What the Choir is searching for is the authentic.

In a recent *New Yorker* profile of American Baptists, the congregation's leadership resigned itself to the fact that "secular culture" would always be "hostile" to Christianity. I don't believe this is true. Our culture is hostile only to the inauthentic living of the gospel. It sniffs out hypocrisy everywhere and knows when Christians aren't taking seriously, what Jesus took seriously. It is, by and large, hostile to the right things. It actually longs to embrace the gospel of inclusion and nonviolence, of compassionate love and acceptance. Even atheists cherish such a prospect.

Human beings are settlers, but not in the pioneer sense. It is our human occupational hazard to settle for little. We settle for purity and piety when we are being invited to an exquisite holiness. We settle for the fear-driven when love longs to be our engine. We settle for a puny, vindictive God when we are being nudged always closer to this wildly inclusive, larger-than-any-life God. We allow our sense of God to atrophy. We settle for the illusion of separation when we are endlessly asked to enter into kinship with all. The Choir has settled for little . . . and the "barking," like a protective sheepdog, wants to guide us back to the expansiveness of God's own longing.

The Choir is certainly more than "the Church." And in many ways, Homeboy Industries is called to be *now*, what the world is called to be ultimately. The Choir understands this. Homeboy wants to give rise not only to the idea of redemptive second chances but also to a new model of church as a community of inclusive kinship and tenderness. The Choir consists of those people who want to Occupy Everywhere, not just Wall Street, and seek, in the here and now, what the world is ultimately designed to become. The Choir, at the end of its living, hopes to give cause to those folks from the Westboro Baptist Church . . . to protest at their funeral.

The Choir aims to stand with the most vulnerable, directing their care to the widow, the orphan, the stranger, and the poor. Those in the Choir want to be taught at the feet of the least. And they want to be caught up in a new model that topples an old order, something wildly subversive and new.

Begin with a title and work backward.

It's been more than thirty years since I first met Dolores Mission Church as pastor and ultimately came to watch Homeboy Industries, born in that poor, prophetic community in 1988, evolve into the largest gang intervention, rehab, and reentry program on the planet. Homeboy has similarly helped 147 programs in the United States and 16 programs outside the country find their beginnings in what we call the Global Homeboy Network.

As in my previous book, *Tattoos on the Heart: The Power of Boundless Compassion*, the essays presented here, again, draw upon three decades of daily interaction with gang members as they jettison their gang past for lives more full in freedom, love, and a bright reimagining of a future for themselves.

I'll try not to repeat myself.

I get invited to give lots of talks: workshops, keynote addresses, luncheon gigs. YouTube is the bane of my existence. I can go to, say, the University of Findlay in Ohio, or Calvin College in Grand Rapids—two places I've never been before—and there will be a handful of folks who've "heard that story before." It happens. I was invited once to give the keynote at an annual gathering of Foster Grandparents in Southern California. I had spoken at the same event the summer before. Virtually the same people, and I'm not sure why they invited me back two summers in a row. After my talk, a grandmother approaches me. I think she liked the talk—there were big tears in her eyes. She grabs both my hands in hers and says, with great emotion, "I heard you last year." She pauses to compose herself. "It never gets better." I suppose I'm delusional in thinking she misspoke.

Anyway, I'll try not to repeat myself.

I can't think, breathe, or proceed—ever—without stories, parables, and wisdom gleaned from knowing these men and women who find their way into our headquarters on the outskirts of Chinatown. We are in the heart of Los Angeles, representing the heart of Los Angeles, and always wanting to model and give a foretaste of the kinship that is God's dream come true. Homeboy Industries doesn't just want to join a dialogue—it wants to create it. It wants to keep its aim true, extol the holiness of second chances, and jostle our mind-sets when they settle for less. As a homie told me once, "At Homeboy, our brand has a heartbeat."

In all my years of living, I have never been given greater access to the tenderness of God than through the channel of the thousands of homies I've been privileged to know. The day simply won't ever come when I am nobler or more compassionate or asked to carry more than these men and women.

Jermaine came to see me, released after more than twenty years in prison. He is a sturdy African American gang member now in his mid-forties. His demeanor is gentle and so, so kind. As I'm speaking with him, I ask if he's on parole and he says yes. Then I ask, "High control?" He nods affirmatively. "I hope you don't mind me asking this: How did someone as kind and gentle and tender as you end up . . . on high-control parole?" Jermaine pauses, then says meekly, "Rough childhood?" Both his manner and words make us laugh. His mom was a prostitute and his father was killed when Jermaine, the oldest of three brothers, was nine. After his father's funeral, his mother rented an apartment, deposited all the boys there, walked to the door, and closed it. They never saw her again. In the many months that followed, Jermaine would take his two younger siblings and sit on the stoop of neighbors' porches. When the residents would inquire, he'd say simply: "We ain't leavin' till ya feed us." We ended our conversation that day with him telling me: "I've decided to be loving and kind in the world. Now . . . just hopin' . . . the world will return the favor."

In the pages that follow are the lives of men and women who have pointed the way for me. For my part, to sit at their feet, has been nothing short of salvific.

I can't write essays about things that matter to me without filling them with God, Jesus, and the gospel rubbing shoulders with stories, snapshots, parables, and wisdom from "the barrio." Also, there is here a regular infusion of "Ignatian spirituality": being a son of Ignatius myself, all the stories of my life get filtered through this Jesuit lens. I only hope the vignettes, koans, and images won't feel too cobbled, the connections too forced, in the stringing of all this together in my second book.

In these elongated homilies, I want to capture the homies' voices as a window of truth to soften the images of them often portrayed in TV and movies.

I should also say that, as in my last book, I don't mention the name of any gang—they've been the cause of too much sadness— and I've changed all the names of the homies here. People had previously criticized the absence of a glossary and a reluctance to translate the Spanish. Again, here, I'm hopeful that the context and meaning will all become evident. There will be the occasion when I do translate something. I will, from time to time, step back and explain something. For instance, when gang members say "fool," they don't mean anything by it. It roughly means "guy." "Did you see that fool that walked by?" Once Martin came in excited to tell me that he had just gotten hired at White Memorial Hospital.

"Congratulations. What do ya do there?"

"I'm the main fool at the gift shop."

"Wow . . . hey . . . let me know if there's an opening for assistant fool."

In the end, each chapter aspires to connect us to a larger view and to participate in a larger love.

I've learned from giving thousands of talks that you never appeal to the conscience of your audience but, rather, introduce them to their own goodness. I remember, in my earliest days, that I used to be so angry. In talks, in op-ed pieces, in radio interviews, I shook my fist a lot. My speeches would rail against indifference and how the young men and women I buried seemed to matter less in the world than other lives. I eventually learned that shaking one's fist at something doesn't change it. Only love gets fists to open. Only love leads to a conjuring of kinship within reach of the actual lives we live.

When Karen Toshima, a graphic artist on a date, was caught in gang crossfire in Westwood Village in 1988, police were pulled from other divisions in Los Angeles and pumped into this area adjacent to UCLA. Detectives were reassigned from other homicide investigations and directed to this case. A hefty reward was offered for information that would lead to the arrest and conviction of whoever had done this. I would soon be burying eight kids in a three-week period in those early days. No cops were shuffled around, no detectives were reassigned, and certainly no rewards were offered to anyone for anything . . . leading me to think that one life lost in Westwood was worth more than hundreds in the barrio. I ranted and shook my fist a great deal. As of this writing, I have buried exactly 220 young human beings killed because of gang violence. In those early days, I would shake my fist a lot at this disparity.

I think Homeboy Industries has changed the metaphor in Los Angeles when it comes to gangs. It has invited the people who live here to recognize their own greatness and does not accuse them of anything. It beckons to their generosity and lauds them for being "smart on crime" instead of mindlessly tough. It seeks an investment rather than futile and endless incarceration. Both this book and Homeboy Industries do not want to simply "point something out" but rather to try and point the way.

Thomas Wolfe, in *You Can't Go Home Again,* writes, "To lose the earth you know, for greater knowing; to lose the life you have for greater life; to leave the friends you loved, for greater loving; to find a land more kind than home, more large than earth." We have to "lose" and "leave"—"unless the grain of wheat dies . . ." The kinship of God won't come unless we shake things up—to "lose the earth you know"—to bark up the wrong tree, and to propose something new.

"Barking" declares that the real world is not what it is cracked up to be. At Homeboy Industries, we don't prepare for the real world—we challenge it. For the opposite of the "real world" is not the "unreal world" but the kinship of God. Therein lies our authenticity as people of faith and card-carrying members of the human race. In this authentic take, survival of the fittest is displaced by the survival of the "unfittest." Cherry-picking makes way for "reverse cherry-picking." What if we ceased to pledge our allegiance to the bottom line and stood, instead, with those who line the bottom? Us versus Them . . . or just Us? Good people/bad people . . . or just God's people? Judgment or awe? Not some accepted/some rejected? . . . No . . . the rejected—the widow, orphan, stranger—are to be favored.

Homeboy Industries (and this book) wants to bend the world to grace, and it doesn't need to turn up the volume in order to accomplish that. It aspires to put a human face on the gang member. If this doesn't happen then kinship is impeded. It is also meant to soften our conventional take on who this gang member is and ushers in an abiding belief that we belong to each other. It is anchored in the truth that all demonizing is untruth.

When we opened Homegirl Café on East First Street eight years ago and the wildly colorful sign sat above the front door, a woman I didn't know called me screaming, "Why would you name it such a thing? You have ruined our neighborhood." Oscar Romero wrote: "A church that doesn't provoke any crises, a gospel that doesn't unsettle, a word of God that doesn't get under anyone's skin, a word that doesn't touch the real sin of the society in which it is being proclaimed—what gospel is that?" It would seem not to take much these days, to provoke or unsettle.

A theme that runs throughout the entire biblical narrative is that God enters our midst to upset the status quo—precisely to bark up the wrong tree. The Magnificat, in Luke's gospel—where the powerful are brought low and the hungry filled with good things—was seen as so subversive that the government of Guatemala, at one time, banned its public recitation. But the truth is, my own tiny-spirited, puny self accommodates the status quo all the time. We adapt, we conform, and we reconfigure everything so that the status quo feels welcome and at home.

When I lived in Bolivia, over thirty years ago, I contracted a bug—a "*bichu*," as they called it . . . that wanted to live in me. It did not want to upset the apple cart, so this bug didn't send me to the bathroom with violent, "both ends" activity. It wanted to live at peace with me. My only symptom was that I lost forty pounds

Introduction

(I'm thinking of returning to Bolivia). The status quo doesn't want things to get upset. But hidden in this détente is division, polarity, and the striking of the high moral distance that separates us. How do we awaken from the dream of separateness, from an abiding sense that the chasm that exists between us cannot be reconciled? For it would seem that the gulf in our present age could not be wider between "Us" and "Them." How do we tame this status quo that lulls us into blindly accepting the things that divide us and keep us from our own holy longing for the mutuality of kinship—a sure and certain sense that we belong to each other?

———

Having said all this, this book feels more playful than not. Like talks I've been inclined to give lately, they feel more like "stand-up" than "stand up to"—getting folks to laugh rather than calling people to some grim duty. But I don't want to become the Art Linkletter of the gang world: "Gang members say the darndest things!" For me, however, it's all about delighting. I enjoy their company, for it is light and affectionate, and charming and good for the soul. To be with them ignites the contagion of God's own tenderness. I never once feel them less than bright, wise, and courageous . . . even when they deal with things painful and unfamiliar. Few gang members are well educated, and yet their core intelligence and insights aren't diminished by this lack. The laughter is never at their expense but seeks to broaden the welcome we all must offer each other.

Besides, it's not for nuthin' that Pope Francis speaks of the "Joy of the Gospel." Once the following of Jesus becomes a strain and a dour, odious task, a "dangerous" job ("somebody's got to do it"), it's lost its way. Once discipleship morphs into the deadly serious and unsmilingly grim, would it not be safe to say that we've wandered far from the gospel's delighting heart?

———

Barking to the Choir

A woman, a volunteer at a very large probation camp, invites the designated kid to come up and do the first reading at mass. The gym is packed with hundreds of minors. "Pablo will now do the first reading," she intones. Pablo still needs to be beckoned with the flick of her hand, and though he has no doubt been previously selected to do this reading, he seems unusually tentative and hesitant. He gets to the podium, and I'm standing next to him, to assist, as I always do, with the occasionally difficult word. He stares blankly at the page, then at the microphone, and then turns to me and whispers, "Out loud?" "Well, um . . . yeah," I say. "That's . . . kind of the idea."

We want to live our lives "out loud"—for all the world to see—not with the volume cranked high but with our lives speaking for themselves.

Kinship is the game-changer. It is the Pearl of Great Price. It is the treasure buried in the field. Let's sell everything to get it. Yet we think kinship is beyond our reach . . . *más allá de esta vida*. Yet Gospel Kinship always exposes the game, jostles the status quo in constant need of conversion, because the status quo is only interested in incessant judging, comparisons, measuring, scapegoating, and competition. And we, the Choir, are stuck in complacency.

I need this conversion. That's why I'm writing about it.

Our settling is a sleeping from which we are asked to awaken. I met some magicians from Magicians Without Borders, who go to refugee camps and the Third World and desperate communities and speak the language of magic. They wanted to bring the same ministry to Homeboy. The currency of magic, they told me, was "appear, disappear, and change." This describes much of the pedagogy of Homeboy Industries and the stuff of attachment repair. They sold the idea to me based on a principle of Harry Houdini's. Houdini felt that the purpose of magic was not just to amaze and amuse. It also sought to awaken hope that the impossible was indeed possible. Not bad. Why settle for less?

Introduction

At Homeboy Industries, thousands and thousands of rival gang members—men and women—have worked in our nine social enterprises: Homeboy Bakery, Homeboy Silkscreen and Embroidery, Homeboy/Homegirl Merchandising, Homeboy Diner (the only place to buy food in the Los Angeles City Hall), Homeboy Café at Los Angeles International Airport, Homeboy Farmers Markets, Homeboy Grocery (a line of food products), Homeboy Recycling, and Homegirl Café and Catering. I'd like to think that if Jesus had more time on this earth, he might well have explored the entrepreneurial. Maybe a clothing line: the Leper Colony, or the Tax Collector's Café, or the Ritually Impure Maintenance Crew. Beyond cure and healing, Jesus was always hopeful about widening the circle of compassion and dismantling the barriers that exclude. He stood with the sinner, the leper, and the ritually impure to usher in some new remarkable inclusion, the very kinship of God. Living the gospel, then, is less about "thinking outside the box" than about choosing to live in this ever-widening circle of inclusion.

At Homegirl Café, women with records, young ladies from rival gangs, and waitresses with attitude will gladly take your order (and they cater). At lunch, the place can be packed with celebs, elected officials, and the powerful "who's who" of Los Angeles. Nearly all the Dodgers came one day for lunch. It was pandemonium. Jim Carrey has dined there several times and it's always a *manicomio*—a madhouse. Joe Biden (and a motorcade) unexpectedly landed for lunch. I was out of town. Afterward, a homie is debriefing me. "While you were gone, we were visited by an MVP." "Do you mean," I ask, "A VIP?" "Yeah, dat one." Then he adds, "Imagine, G: here at Homeboy, we were visited by the Vice President of the United States . . . MICK ROMNEY." (File this under "All white guys look alike.") We may need to add some current-affairs classes to our curriculum.

Diane Keaton came in for lunch one day with a regular, weekly customer. The Oscar-winning Keaton is greeted by her waitress,

Glenda. She is a big girl who has just spent a long stint in a California state prison. Glenda is tattooed, a felon, a gang member, and on parole. Glenda does not know who Diane Keaton is. She hands the movie star her menu, and Keaton asks her waitress, "What do YOU recommend?" Glenda rattles off the three *platillos* ("dishes") she particularly likes and Keaton makes her pick. "I'll have that second one. That sounds good."

It's at this point that something suddenly dawns on Glenda. "Wait a minute," she says, bouncing her finger in Diane Keaton's direction. "I feel like I know you. Like . . . maybe we've met." The actress quickly and humbly seeks to deflect Glenda's notice. "Oh . . . I suppose . . . I have one of those faces . . . that people think they've seen before." Glenda ignites in a burst of recognition. "No . . . wait . . . now I know . . . WE WERE LOCKED UP TOGETHER!"

That took my breath away when I heard it. And I don't believe we've had any further Diane Keaton sightings, now that I think of it. But suddenly . . . kinship so quickly. Oscar-winning actress. Attitudinal waitress. Exactly what God had in mind. And I suppose, in order to know that mind, we need go no further than Jesus speaking to the gathered when he expresses his deepest longing: "that . . . you . . . may . . . be . . . one." I suppose he could have been more self-referential. But it would seem that Jesus wants this to be about "us" and our willingness, eventually, to connect to each other. So the Choir gets barked at and, collectively, we move beyond the mind we have. And with enough jostling and juggling, we find ourselves anchored in God's dream come true.

Finally unsettled—connected to each other, entering kinship . . . now!

CHAPTER ONE

The Dude Shows Up

God is a nudge. Not in the nagging, annoying sense, but in a gentle, leaning-into sense. It is indeed a challenge to abandon the long-held belief that God yearns to blame and punish us, ask us to measure up or express disappointment and disapproval at every turn. It is part of our hardwiring. But we can feel, nonetheless, God nudging us beyond our tired, atrophied complacence toward something more oceanic and spacious. We feel God's desire for fullness to dwell in us. We are always being pushed and inched closer to the "God who is always greater," as Saint Ignatius frames it. Or as a homie changing gears in his head from Spanish to English awkwardly but accurately blurts, "God is Big."

We want to believe that we have a God, as Hafez asserts, who only knows four words.

Every child has known God.
Not the God of names,
Not the God of don'ts,
Not the God who ever does anything weird.
But the God who only knows
Four words.
And He keeps repeating them, saying:
"Come dance with me."
Come
Dance.

In spite of God's magnitude, we have managed successfully to domesticate God. Beg. Roll over. We prefer God tamed and ready to do OUR bidding. We have trained God, if you will, to "do God's business" outside. No doubt though, God wants to be found in the mess inside. We have settled for a "partial God," as Richard Rohr puts it, when every minute of every moment we are asked to "move beyond the mind we have" and land increasingly on a renewed and expansive view of God. We are human beings, so we endlessly create God in our own image. We can't help ourselves. But certainly we can catch ourselves.

Gang members are forever contorting the English language in what I call "homie-propisms." A homegirl wants to introduce her "man" to me and presents him as "my sufficient other." No doubt. A trainee came into my office one morning and says, "Damn, G. My lady . . . she's in a BAD mood today." When I ask why, he says that she's beginning her "administration period." I tell him that, with the arrival of a new CEO to take over my duties, I've just finished my own and know what she's going through.

I was once saying mass at the San Fernando Juvenile Hall. With nearly three hundred detained minors—mostly gang members—a homie reads from Psalm 138. I'm seated, vested, eyes closed, choosing to listen to this kid's proclamation, rather than follow along in the liturgical sheet that rests on my lap. He reads, with an over-abundance of confidence, "The Lord . . . is EXHAUSTED." *What the hell?* I open my eyes and hurriedly refer to my sheet. It says, "The Lord is exalted," but I think "exhausted" is way better. I'm not sure I want to spend eternity with a God who wants to be exalted, who longs to be recognized and made a big deal of. I would rather hope for a humble God who gets exhausted in delighting over and loving us. That is a better God than the one we have.

All of us have had conversations with friends in which we ask how they're doing and they respond, "I'm so tired. But it's a good tired." Then they will tell you how they spent the day helping a friend move into her apartment or the weekend watching their grandkids. It's a "good" tired because it was spent in extension to another. The exhausted God is always greater than the exalted one.

One day a homie comes into my office with his five-year-old son. "He's got a question for ya." The kid looks at me and sidles closer, nervous but determined.

"Does God have hair and does he wear a robe?"

I look him in the eye. "Yes, and only when he steps out of the shower."

God, of course, is unchanging and immutable. But our sense of who God is changes as we grow and experience God, and God is constantly nudging us toward that evolution. It is true enough that my image of God at five years old is not the one I have today. And if that's true, why wouldn't my sense of God be different ten minutes from now and twenty minutes after that?

God leans into us so that we will let go of the image of God as unreasonable parent, exacting teacher, or ruthless coach. God is not who we think God is. Our search for God is not a scavenger hunt; God is everywhere and in everything. Our sense of God always beckons us to grow, to reimagine something wildly more breathtaking than where our imagination generally takes us. We are nudged toward an increasingly wider view and image of God from our child consciousness to an adult consciousness. God leans into us so that we can find our way to this inner absorption of God. With any luck and some attention, we will keep landing on a better God, finally having grown comfortable in God's tenderness. Our God is constantly saying, "*Ándale*" . . . "Go ahead."

We refine our sense, then, of God and what Ignatius calls the "Magis," which refers to an affection for God. He also calls it "devotion," which is a pervasive familiarity and union with God, a desire to want what God wants. We seek to live where God is and our understanding of that evolves and changes all the time. This is consequential for, as Jesus says, "Come to me and you'll find rest." We are not being offered sleep, but freedom. There is an openness—the spacious, expansive, inclusive heart to which we are invited. "*Ándale*."

The vast majority of homies who come to us at Homeboy have histories of trauma, which can lead to disorganized attachment patterns. Mom, typically the primary caregiver, was either frightened or frightening—and the idea of her (or whoever has occupied that role) can trigger both "approach" and "avoidance" at the same time. Wanting to move toward and flee this person can lead to dissociative symptoms later on in life. Attachment repair, then, is the order of the day at Homeboy Industries as gang members seek to "reidentify" themselves. Arrival at the heart of God is often impeded by one's own history of trauma. This healthier sense of God may be achieved through a concept called "object constancy," the capacity to hold on to the existence or "sense" of the caregiver, even when the caregiver is not physically present.

One of our therapists told me of arriving to work on a Monday with a box of Triscuits for one of her clients, Andres, who is always "hongry," as he puts it. As a nine-year-old, he came home from school to find that his mother (whom I presume was mentally ill) had packed up her things and left her only son. For the next two years he was homeless and a Dumpster diver, sleeping on park benches until he was found by the "system." After foster care, gang involvement, and detention, Andres wandered into our place and began our program.

"You brought these for me?" he asked in disbelief. The therapist told me later that he was stunned that she had "held" him all weekend.

She nodded.

"You mean . . . you think of me . . . when you're not here?"

She nodded again.

"Wow. I never pictured that anyone would think of me when they're not here."

Without optimal care-giving relationships and object constancy, the gang members who walk through our doors can feel real anguish and abandonment. There is a chronic fear of both intimacy and being left behind. "I will never forget you," Isaiah has God say to us for this exact reason. And truth be told about our God: God thinks of us even when we don't think God's there.

Years ago, when I was a chaplain at Folsom State Prison, I met an inmate named "the Fat Man." Every day he would ask me to walk around the yard with him. "Let's do a few laps," he'd say. He was a huge bear of a man, with an unruly Rasputin beard. The Fat Man was roughly my age and had spent most of his life in prison, becoming greatly involved in the politics of the place. He was now on the tail end of finishing a very long sentence. All his adult life he had been a heroin addict, even in prison, but now he was sober and reflective. He'd talk and talk of God on these walks, and our "sessions" would always end the same way. He'd say, "Who loves ya, baby?" and wrap his arms around me. Then he would add, "Don't forget, G. I love ya like a rock."

Shortly after his release, the Fat Man died. A rekindled acquaintance with heroin was more than his body could take. I presided at his funeral, and when I mentioned his "Love ya like a rock" refrain, all the heads in the congregation nodded in recognition. Apparently he said it to everyone. For years I appropriated the phrase. Many letters to locked-up homies would end with it, as would conversations, to the point that it became expected, even after a straightforward lecture. "I know, I know," they'd say, with a great rolling of their eyes. "Ya love me like a rock." I couldn't help it.

Hafez gives us this image: "God and I have become like two giant fat people living in a tiny boat. We keep bumping into each other and laughing." This feels like the pulse of God to me—to be loved like a rock, forever, unchanging, and as solid as can be. We need to let ourselves be bumped into and loved by the Fat Man. God hopes that the laughing will be contagious.

A homie named Rogelio and his six-year-old son, Arturo, are in the public pool on a very hot August day. There are countless "cannonballs" and Arturo's endless rounds of "Do it again" at whatever thing Arturo finds delightful and wants his dad to repeat. Rogelio, after years of gang involvement, is trying his unsteady hand at fatherhood and earning clean money. It is a suit that is beginning to fit him.

Rogelio asks for a respite from the "Do it agains" and flops down on his towel at the edge of the pool. Little Arturo swims toward his father and folds his arms at the pool's lip, facing him. They don't speak. Rogelio is lying on his stomach and sees that his kid's face is but two feet away from his. Finally, Arturo says, "*Apa*, when I have a son I want to be a dad just like you."

When Rogelio tells me the story over the phone, this last line silences him. I wait. "What are you feeling right now, *mijo*?" I ask.

Rogelio pauses. Then, voice cracking, he says, "Chills."

The very pulse of God.

During Advent, we are called to prepare the way . . . to "make straight the path" and make smooth what is rocky. Our hardwiring is such that we hear these invitations as a demand to "straighten up" or "get our act together." But it's not we who needs changing—it's our crooked path that needs to be smoothed . . . so we can be reached by God's tenderness. One of the many impediments to hearing the only message God longs to communicate to us is our marriage to the pain we carry and the lament that accompanies it. With grace, we come to know that lament can't get a foothold if gratitude gets there first.

A homie named Cuco bursts excitedly into my office at the end of the workday with a book he is reading in our fatherhood class. He opens it to a page he has marked, and I see that there is only one sentence underlined. He reads it to me: "Fatherhood is an adventure." It's an unremarkable sentence, and I ask him why he's underlined it. Cuco sits down in a chair across from my desk. He's in his early twenties and his demeanor is open and always ready for joy. "Well, cuz every night when I get home, my four-year-old son rushes me at the door, flings his arms around my legs, and hugs me. Then he asks, 'You know what time it is?' And I always say, 'No, what time is it?' And he throws out his arms and says, 'It's time . . . for an ADVEN . . . TUUUURRRE.' He always says it the same way: 'AN ADVEN . . . TUUUURRRE.'" I ask him if he taught his son the word. "I have no idea where he got it from," he answers. "Cartoons, I guess." His smile is unable to relax the hold it has on his soul. "And every day I gotta think up some crazy-ass adventure for the two of us."

I ask Cuco another question, though I'm not sure why. "Did you know your father?"

"Nope," he says, the regret of that truth unable to wobble his delight. "Never met him." His smile remains. Not a rock in the path. Mountains reduced to a plain so the tenderness can get right to you.

———

One gorgeous morning at Camp David Gonzales, one of the juvenile probation camps where I say mass, I see a kid I don't know standing by himself, just staring at the Santa Monica Mountains. I ask how he's doing.

"Well," he says, "I'm a little low on faith." This seems like an odd place to start, as the homies say, "right out da gate." But then he adds quickly, "You know what I do when I'm low on faith?"

I shake my head and lean in. My faith's gas tank has been known to hover at "E," so I wanted to know.

"I stand right here and I look at them mountains," he says. "I stare at the blue sky and white clouds. I breathe in this clean air." He demonstrates all of this. "Then I say to myself, 'God did this.'" He turns to me, with some emotion and a surfeit of peace. "And I know everything will be all right." The open-handed thrill of knowing what God wants us to know.

I'm reminded of Beto, a gang member in our training program who once took his young son to Griffith Park for a pony ride. For some reason his kid was terrified and had a total meltdown, refusing to go near the animal. Some weeks later, Beto took the boy back—not to force him to ride but to show him that, whatever happened, Beto was with him and he would keep him safe. This time the boy got on the pony and rode knowing he was not alone, soothed in tenderness and comforted by the feeling that everything would be all right.

I have this red string tied around my wrist, a gift from the Dalai Lama. His Holiness blessed it by holding it in his hand, then up to his forehead, then blowing on it. The string has a knot in it—not where I've tied it to my wrist, but located in the center of the string somehow. Over the course of the day, the knot works its way to the side of my wrist, and I'm constantly moving the knot back to my wrist's center. The knot represents the God who I long to be at the center of my life. It helps me remain restful in that center—unable to think of myself except in terms of God. It returns me to the stillness there. "Let us . . . strive to enter into that rest," we read in Hebrews, knowing that this is never an end in itself but equips us to follow Jesus and create the kind of kinship about which God dreams. It is not sleep.

On a visit to another probation camp, I see Brian, a sixteen-year-old who worked at Homeboy for a time but then disappeared. When he sees me, he is so excited, he vacates his skin. This often happens when you encounter a kid whom you have known on the streets: you become a touchstone, a slice of home, and the recognizable. He wraps me up in a bear hug and won't let go.

We talk for some time and I'm struck by how much Brian's matured. His conversation is thoughtful and measured in a way only adults can pull off. I tell him how impressed I am with his transformation. He admits (as many often do) that maybe getting locked up was not the worst thing that ever happened to him. Then suddenly he makes an abrupt lane change.

"I pray a lot," he says, nodding. "I just love to pray."

Brian isn't telling me something he thinks I want to hear. It's clear that this impulse in him is genuine and heartfelt, and born of his daily experience in this facility.

I ask him to tell me more about his newfound relationship with God. He seems startled by the question yet thrilled that I would want to know how he sees things.

"It's great," he gushes, lighting up with a smile. Then, almost as suddenly, he's completely overwhelmed. He pulls his hands to his face and begins to cry. In prayer he has found release. As a Folsom inmate put it, "grabbin' God's outstretched hand and goin' for a walk."

Come dance with me.

A question I'm always asked during the Q and A sessions after my talks is if I have ever come close to losing my faith. People ask this, I presume, because I have buried 220 kids, all killed because of gang violence—kids I loved, often killed by kids I love. I am never quite certain what this question means or how to answer it. I never shake my fist at God after tragedy. After all, what did God have to do with it? I'm never inclined to see God as an accomplice (or, as gang members who attend Criminals & Gang Members Anonymous meetings call it, "God as crime partner").

Some people say, "God is good, and God has a plan for you." I believe that God is good but also that God is too busy loving me to have a plan for me. Like a caring parent, God receives our childlike painting of a tree—usually an unrecognizable mess—and delights in it. God doesn't hand it back and say, "Come back when it looks more like a tree" or tell us how to improve it. God simply delights in us. Like the kid at probation camp after confession: "You mean you just sealed my record?" The God who always wants to clean the slate is hard to believe. Yet the truth about God is that God is too good to be true. And whenever human beings bump into something too good to be true, we decide it's not true.

In a correspondence with a priest in Ireland, Jackie Kennedy wrote that she felt bitter toward God after the assassination of her husband. "How could God let this happen?" she asked. But God wasn't in the Texas School Book Depository, aiding and abetting. God was—and is—in the heartbreak and in the insight born of sadness, and in the arms that wrap around our grief. I have felt this every time a kid is gunned down. Or when you have to lay off three hundred of your workers because you can't meet payroll. Or when you are given a cancer diagnosis. Such things don't shake your faith—they shape it.

Some things are random and other things are meant to be in our control. So God is with me when "shit happens" and God is rooting for me when I need to decide things. And I'm okay with that. I don't need God to be in charge of my life. I only need God to be at the center of it.

Over twenty years ago, when Homeboy Industries was still called "Jobs for a Future," we had payday every Friday. We employed nearly sixty former gang members at the time and funds were so low that I was writing more bad checks than a member of Congress. (Once a homie told me he had seen the movie "*101 Donations*." I asked him, "Why didn't you invite me?") As Friday was looming, I found myself needing $10,000—otherwise I'd be handing out IOUs. I was entering the panic zone, so preoccupied with worry that it became difficult to attend to my duties as pastor. The day before payday, a woman pulled up to the front of the parish office in what the homies would call a "bucket," ignoring the designated parking signs. She said that it was urgent that she speak with me, so she was brought into my office. She was in her late seventies, dressed not too differently from a bag lady, layered and oddly arrayed. Her husband had recently died, she explained, and she had been cleaning his room. "He always respected what you do with gang members," she said as she passed me a very worn paper bag wrapped around itself twice. She explained that she had found it under his mattress. I unwound the bag and found a stack of bills inside. "I stopped counting," she said, "once I got to $10,000." I didn't. It was $12,000.

As elated as I was, I had no need to believe that God had orchestrated this woman's arrival. God would have been centrally present even if I had to face down some very bereft homies. After all, nothing depends on how things turn out—only on how you see them when they happen. Emmanuel: the name that means God with us is not moving the dials and turning the switches but tenderly holding us through it all.

Everyone gets those emails . . . usually sent from strangers. There is this particular one that made the rounds that recounts how all these people, heading to the World Trade Center on 9/11, were delayed arriving because of some small annoyance. Traffic jam due to an accident on the New Jersey Turnpike. A kid's first day in kindergarten. My turn to get the donuts for the office. The alarm didn't go off. The list is long. The writer concludes that though we are initially frustrated by such derailments, they remain proof that God is at work watching over us. Then we have to believe that God, on 9/11, watched over some and failed to watch over thousands of others. Which then paints us into a preposterous corner, forcing us to say, "God has his reasons," or, worse, "Heaven needed another angel." I believe that God protects me from nothing but sustains me in everything.

I once gave an evening talk at a private school in Los Angeles. The place was packed with parents and a handful of students. Sitting in the front row was my friend Vivienne. Her husband, Rey, had invited me to speak. Beside her was her ten-year-old son, Diego. Throughout my talk, I kept noticing Diego. Though he was young, he was mature beyond his years, bright and articulate, without an ounce of ten-year-old fidget. As I spoke, he hung on every word, laughing at all the right places and dropping his jaw when things got more serious. I finished my talk with a heartbreaking story of Puppet and Youngster, sworn enemies who became brothers while working together until Puppet was beaten to death. Suddenly, Diego was sobbing. Even as I continued to speak on auto-pilot, I kept observing him, astonished at his reaction. Puppet's untimely death had so affected Diego that he was experiencing a full-bodied sorrow, heaving and rocking in his seat. Vivienne turned to him and slowly, sweetly, put her arm around him. What Diego did next is, quite literally, a showstopper. He reared up and at full volume screamed at his Mom: "WHAT?" I stop speaking. Everyone turned and looked. He demurred, but only a little. He leaned in again, and repeated in a fairly loud stage whisper: "WHHHAAAATTTT?" It was clear that he was asking "What?" as in *WHAT have I done now? HOW have I disappointed you now?*

It could be true that Vivienne simply wanted to settle her kid down, since everyone was looking at him. And yet her expression seemed to ask, *How did I get so lucky to have such a son?* But she is also heartbroken by the very thing that breaks the heart of her kid.

She wanted to console him and let him know that he was not alone. This mother did not want "from" him. She only wanted "for" him.

Often enough, we get in the habit of shaking our fists at God and saying, *WHAT do you WANT from me?* We are programmed this way as humans. But I suppose it would be more accurate to ask God this: *What do you want FOR me?* For starters: life, happiness, and peace: My joy yours. Your joy complete. That's it. Nothing less than that.

When it comes to the masses I say at probation camps, some are less formal than others. Instead of following the written prayers of petition or the intentions, I often invite the gathered kids to spontaneously offer their prayers for the things on their mind and in their hearts. I begin by providing a model. "For our communities, so often plagued by violence, that we will choose to be ambassadors of peace . . . let us pray to the Lord." Then everyone says, "Lord, hear our prayer." I do three of these then encourage the congregation to share their own. The homies often can be very generous. One kid prays: "For Father Greg . . . that he get home safe today." When I thank him afterward and tell him that his prayer made me feel good, he answers, with surprising and immediate tears, that it made him feel good to say it. Another time a guy in the front row, something of a leader at the camp, contributes, "For my homie, Lefty, that when he goes home this week, he does good and doesn't get in any more trouble." Then he flounders a bit, unclear how to end this thing. Before I can insert "Let us pray to the Lord," he supplies his own rendition. "Pretty much it." He offers three more petitions all ending with "Pretty much it." The troops like his version better than mine: every prayer that follows ends with "Pretty much it."

We are forever fretting over things we think ruffle God's feathers. God is not feathered, though. A homie said to me once, "I think God has disowned me." But Wisdom writes, "You love all things that are and loathe nothing." Why is that so hard for us to digest?

We are always trying to "make a good impression," but God is not so interested. Dressed for a job interview, a homie once told me: "I just want to make a good expression." That's more like it. Our lives, fully expressive of God's pleasure, delight, and loving-kindness.

Pretty much it.

Hector has his four young kids for the weekend and takes them to the Central Library on a Saturday morning. The kiddie floor is a little crazy, so he takes a couple of books and leads his crew to the adult section, which is nearly empty. They plant themselves in a corner on plush, spacious leather chairs, the kids' little legs barely reaching the ends of the chair's cushions. Hector, both a recovering gang member and heroin addict, begins to read in a hushed tone. But he notices the librarian, a gentleman in his thirties standing behind a desk, giving him what he thinks is the hairy eyeball. Hector feels a flush of self-consciousness. *Maybe I shouldn't be here,* he thinks to himself, feeling judged. He finishes the two books, corrals his gaggle of four, and makes for the door. But the librarian waves him over. Hector, readies himself to be chewed out for reading to kids in the adult area. He situates his kids at a distance, in case what the librarian says takes everybody south for a second. But the librarian only looks kindly at Hector, smiles, and says simply, "Good job."

When I first began to preach at Dolores Mission, I would write out the homilies, in my halt and lame Spanish, then have some native speaker go over it for me. The message was always a variation on a central theme: God is too busy loving you to have any time left over to be disappointed. I sought to comfort the afflicted and fill them with the utter fullness of God. But people would leave the church after mass, shake my hand, and then shake their heads, pleading with me, *"Regáñanos, padre."* Chew us out. I soon realized that this is what the people had come to expect from their priests: a full-blown accounting of how disappointing they were, always failing to measure up to God's high expectations.

When we are disappointed in each other, we least resemble God. We have a God who wonders what all the measuring is about, a God who is perplexed by our raising the bar and then raising it even higher. We would do well to ask ourselves, *How does God handle dismay and disappointment?* Surely God must be disappointed that hunger exists in the world when we have the means to feed everyone. God has to be saddened by the number of guns in the United States and people's willingness to use them on each other. God undoubtedly is dismayed that the Catholic Church continues to exclude women from ordained ministry and limit gays and the divorced and remarried Catholic from the fullest of welcomes. One can only imagine God's response to the Church's global child abuse scandal. But in all this, and in many other things, disappointment is not the foot God puts forward. There is instead only a redoubling of God's loving us into kinship with each other. If we truly allow that tenderness to reach us, then peace, justice, and equality will be its by-product.

A homie, locked up in a Youth Authority facility, wrote me: "I really want to change but every night I pray for God to come into my life but it's not happening. Here's how I see it sometimes. I see it this way . . . I try to talk to God but it's like he's got a Walkman on and his headphones and he's bumping some oldies and he can't hear my prayer." Sometimes we just presume radio silence from God because we deem ourselves so disappointing to him.

"There's a wideness in God's mercy," the old hymn proclaims. In order to experience this mercy and love, we need to accept that there is room for us in it. God loves us whole and entire, and as a community, if we emulate that, then hunger, weaponry, inequality, and every other evil will dissipate into obsolescence. This can only come when I know that I am accepted especially at my worst. A homie named Eddie explains it this way: "God is that person pushing the shopping cart and going through your garbage. Sometimes we don't want him to go through our garbage, but he tells us that he wants to. That's how it is, I think. God holds our garbage and recycles it into love."

———

A seventeen-year-old homie, fresh out of probation camp, comes to see me a week after his release. He asks me if I remember giving him a gift card for clothes a few days earlier. I do. He tells me that he's lost it. "And I suppose," I ask, messing with him, "you want me to give you another one?" He waves this off. "No . . . that would be ridic– . . . COULD YOU?" We are all being invited into the roominess of God's generosity. The wideness awaits us.

Lety, a homegirl who has been through the wringer and then back again, sits snug up to the front of my desk. Name any horrific, terrible thing that could befall a human being and it's befallen her: prison, drug addiction, domestic violence, kids taken away. It would be a far shorter list if you wrote down the horrific things that *haven't* happened to her. In fact, I can't think of anything. I would not have survived one day in her childhood. She's asking me for some help when she suddenly says, "I wish you were God." I laugh, but I see that Lety, a famous *chillona* (crybaby), is starting to well up.

"Why do you wish I was God?" I ask.

She needs time here—for composure, not composition of thought. "Cuz . . . I think you'd let me into heaven."

This blindsides me and now I become a *chillón*. I need my time to formulate a response as my eyes moisten. I grab her hands and pull her as close as I can across the top of my desk. I look her in the eyes. We are both crying. We gaze at each other for a very long time.

"Lety," I begin, "I swear to you, IF I get to heaven and you're not there . . . I'm not stayin'."

The Dude Shows Up

We believe that God is inclined to decline our credit card, that our account with God has insufficient funds. We don't understand God's generosity—it flies in the face of our human allergy to having the wool pulled over our eyes. But God is not who we think God is. A homie once told me, as he was finishing our training program, "I feel like I fell in 'like' with myself here." At Homeboy, I suppose the "task" is attachment repair, but it's really about looking into each other's eyes and pulling each other across the expanse of a desk and seeing what God sees. This generosity with each other is gratuitous and abundant and who God is.

Thumper telephones and tells me he's ready to take his driving test. He wants to use my car. I'm not sure he even knows how to drive, but I make an appointment for him at the DMV and pick him up at his home. I tell him to take the wheel so he can get used to things. Suddenly it's Mr. Toad's Wild Ride. Thumper is, quite simply, the worst driver to ever take a driving test. I'm trying to let him down easy as we pull up to the test site and my car inches closer in line for the next inspector.

"You know, son," I tell him, "I didn't pass my test the first time. So you know, maybe with some more practice . . ." Then I see the inspector walking toward our car with a clipboard and I smile. It's Maria. I've known her family for nearly all her life. She grew up in the projects. I did her *quinceañera* mass. I baptized her kids. I turn to Thumps. "Dog, unless you mow down a pedestrian, you actually may pass this thing."

Maria screams my name when she sees me and asks what I'm doing there. I gesture toward Thumper from the passenger seat. Then she quickly shifts to her professional driving inspector voice.

"Excuse me, sir," she says, winking at me. "If you could please step out of the car." We switch places and they drive away.

I pace in the parking lot for about twenty minutes until I see them walking toward me. They have parked the car some distance away, in the nether region of the property. They aren't speaking. I search for a sign in either one's body language. Thumper sees me and slows his pace so he's a stride behind Maria and she can't see him. He gives me two thumbs up and a full-screen smile. Then he catches up to her. Now it's Maria's turn to decelerate a full body length behind Thumper. She mimes an enormous sigh and, with considerable exaggeration, makes a very elaborate sign of the cross. Maria has wandered into the generous terrain of God.

Generosity in Buddhism is to be relieved of the "stain of stinginess." God thinks there is plenty to go around. Before Homeboy Industries was born, we started an alternative school for middle school–aged gang members. They were wreaking havoc in the projects, and no other school would have them. Our parish convent occupied the entire third floor above our parochial school. I gather these six Belgian nuns in their living room. Their accents were thick and their hearts brilliant. "Hey," I ask, "Would you guys mind . . . you know . . . moving out . . . and we could turn the convent into a school for gang members?" They looked at me, then at each other, and said simply, "Sure." And that was the entirety of their discernment process. No stain of stinginess. The abundance of God breaks through the clouds in a solitary "Sure."

"My love, my dove, my beautiful one."

I hear this at mass one day, in the first reading from the Song of Songs and I think to myself, *So that's where that's from.* Before I was ordained, I taught English at Loyola High School in Los Angeles in the late '70s. Among the thirty or so Jesuits who lived there was an older man named Alphonse Domachowski, a semiretired priest who was chaplain to the Knights of Columbus. He was short and shit-brickhouse built. In his eighties he didn't so much walk as waddle. No one called him "Al"—he was "Chisky." Charlie Gagan, the Jesuit principal of the school, would see Chisky ambling toward us in the long, dark hallways of the Jesuit residence and start singing a modified version of the "Friskies" cat food jingle from the commercial: "Little Chisky, little Chisky . . . ain't we got fun." Chisky's determined waddle became this apoplectic convulsion. Without fail, this routine would slay him. Always. The bit that never got old.

Every morning Chisky would see me walking down the hall in the residence and say with such sweetness and dentures rattling: "My love, my dove, my beautiful one." I never knew it was from Scripture. It gave Chisky permission to tell you—right out loud—that he loved you. God rhyming in the form of an old Polish guy who delights in greeting you the same way every day. God, for whom our jokes never get old, finding us. And we feel reached by the tenderness. The path is smoothed. Pretty much it.

--- ---

Chuy is texting me. He needs help getting a refrigerator.

For a long time he had been a big, bad gang member and drug dealer. "I was disguised as that guy," he told me once. He began in our program as all do, in janitorial services, then he worked in our tattoo removal department. After his eighteen months were up, he moved beyond us, having found a good-paying job with the help of our employment services department. On his last day at Homeboy, he asked to address the gathered at our morning meeting. He directed his remarks to the trainees present.

"All of you," he began, "are diamonds covered in dust."

He choked up a bit.

"You . . . can wipe your dust off here."

In his time with us, he had experienced a true liberation and discovered his truest self. As a colleague at Homeboy said, "Chuy learned how to be loyal to his own life."

It's a Saturday and I'm running from mass to talk to baptism. Chuy's a persistent fellow, though, and after a few messages I text back that he should meet me in the fridge section of Sears at 4:30.

He writes back: "Got it. Meet for Beers at 4:30." "He gots jokes"—as the homies would say.

I find him there, right on time, when I arrive. He gallops toward me, sweeps me up in his arms, and lifts me off the ground in a giant hug. Lots of bystanders stop to stare. When he releases me from his grip, I ask him, "Have they called security on your ass yet?" "Not yet," he answers, "but it's only a matter of time." He lets loose his signature laugh—the kind you would want to bottle and carry with you, releasing squeals of it whenever you needed to be lifted up—and turns to the refrigerator salesman, Edgar, whom he has already befriended. I'm touched as I watch them interact, and before long they make a deal and arrange the delivery.

I drive Chuy home and as we pull up in front of his East Side apartment he tells me that lately he's "been having one-on-ones with . . . you know . . . God."

"I don't understand it," he says as he turns and looks at me. "The Dude shows up." I find this pretty charming and chuckle at first. Then I see that Chuy is as serious as can be. "I mean . . . why would he do that?" he asks, allowing his tears free passage. "After all the shit and bad I've done, why would he show up?"

"Ever since Happiness heard your name," the poet Hafez writes, "it's been running down the street trying to find you." In Wisdom it asks, "Who can conceive what the Lord intends?" No one escapes the notice of God. So we try to find the joy there is in God's finding us. God intends our happiness. We pull up our antennae to its furthest peak and place ourselves on the lookout for glimpses of joy at its most unleashed. The path is cleared and God's own tenderness is locating us. We never stop looking, until we realize that we have already been found. Good job.

Rico was something of a mascot in Homeboy's earliest office. An exceedingly slow kid and the perennial whipping boy for bullies, ten-year-old Rico took the brunt of all kinds of taunting and derision. He would forever call me from the pay phone at Hollenbeck

Junior High, crying that someone had thrown his books away or tossed him in the Dumpster. Frequently his phone calls would get cut off by the bully tormenting him. He found solace and sanctuary in our office. The attention he got from all of us was transformative. Staff would take him on trips to Office Depot, spend time with him, help him know how to tell time and memorize his own birthday. He just couldn't get enough of what everyone lavished on him. The beloved son of Homeboy Industries.

Once, late on a hot, August afternoon, I was celebrating the five o'clock Saturday vigil mass at Dolores Mission. I was in the middle of my homily, standing below the altar, in front of the congregation, when suddenly the side door was flung open loudly. There stood little Rico, a huge smile on his face. I stopped preaching and all eyes turned toward him. He was beaming and giddy with excitement, limbs gyrating every which way.

"Rico," I greeted him. "What's up?"

And, just like that, Rico thrust his arms toward me and said with unbridled joy, "I'm finding you!"

Chills.

CHAPTER TWO

"Holy Befold"

Whenever Gato, a large, burly gang member, is telling a story and approaching the climax, he wants to say "And lo and behold" but says instead "And holy befold." I never correct him, because his version is better than the original—indeed, it is the sacred, the holy, unfolding right before our eyes. We tend to think the sacred has to look a certain way. In our minds, we call central casting to supply cathedral spires, incense, jewel-encrusted chalices, angelic choirs. When imagining the sacred, we think of church sanctuary rather than living room; chalice instead of cup; ordained male priest instead of, well, ourselves. But lo—which is to say, look—right before your eyes, the holy is happening, even if you are hesitant to believe it.

The Psalmist speaks of us wanting to evade or hide from the

love of God. "If I fly to the heavens" or "If I hide in the depths, even there." But in your darkest place, or in what you believe is your most hidden hideousness—even there, God is dwelling. What God considers sacred won't be pigeonholed. As human beings, we find it difficult to recognize the holy as God does. Nothing is outside the realm of sanctity, for the world is infused with God's presence. God has trouble understanding the distinction we make between the sacred and what we believe to be the profane. But that's what human beings do: we confine the divine.

Ignatius of Loyola invites us to find God in all things. And he means *all* things. He is right in saying this, for the world is steeped in God. Grace indeed is everywhere. Ignatius discouraged his Jesuits from meditating on lofty, abstract divine truths. Meditate on the world, he instructed them, and all that happens in it, packed shoulder to shoulder with God. We live amidst a universe soaked in grace that invites us to savor it.

When the homies have clocked out for the day, an informal "salon" sometimes takes place in my office. Conversations bounce all over the place. One time I decided to broach the subject of church, wanting to hear the homies' experience of it. I was curious if any of them had ever had a "religious experience" in a church or in the traditional ways we'd imagine. I was greeted with shrugs and a chorus of "I don't knows." I pressed them, but no one was able to jostle up memories of the sacred.

Then Nestor spoke up.

"Yeah. I remember a time." His large frame quickened to attention. "I was a little kid. Maybe I was in church with my mom, can't remember. But there was this woman down the pew from me. She was the most beautiful woman I had ever seen. Couldn't take my eyes off her. And she had her small son sitting on her lap. All of a sudden, she whipped out her tittie and started to breastfeed her kid. I mean, daaaamn, it was amazing. And I knew, from that moment on, I would always love women for the rest of my life."

Okaaaay, not exactly what I was looking for. I wanted central casting: this homie, alone in prayer in some church, a beam of light streaming through the stained-glass window. Cue the choir of angels. I imagined Nestor tearfully echoing the prophet Samuel, saying, "Speak, Lord, for your servant is listening." But that's not what I got. Instead, I got a real, sure-footed memory of a sacred moment that I could not dismiss. Slowly, then, you begin to learn not to discount the power of a single thing to carry within it supreme holiness.

———

Though the words were not in his toolbox, I knew my father loved me. During my high school years, there were ten of us at home. At breakfast, my younger brother and sisters would take their bowls of Trix into the next room to eat in front of cartoons, while my mom would fuss with the endless loads of laundry. That usually just left my dad and me, eating our Cheerios and reading the *LA Times* in the breakfast room. He would be planted on a short bench at the end of the table, near the windows. I would sit in the middle, bowl tucked in close, paper spread out before me. We wouldn't speak. Perkiness was strictly prohibited. "So, how'd ya sleep last night?" was never a question we asked. *LA Times*. Cheerios. Silence.

When my dad was finished and got up from the table, he'd need to pass behind me. I'd instinctively scoot in my chair so he had room. But before moving past me, he'd place his empty bowl on the table. Then, standing behind me, he'd massage my neck, his thumbs digging deep. He smelled like Fitch shampoo and Aqua Velva aftershave. The massage didn't last long, but he did it every day, wordlessly.

Thirty years later, I'm on a silent retreat in a monastery in the California redwoods, sitting in the chapel and not having a good morning. I'm rehashing old story lines: ancient hurts and resentments. The soreness in my soul is palpable—enveloping me, actually. I'm in a chair in the last row, off to the side. There are huge windows behind me, the massive redwoods visible in the early morning sunlight.

Suddenly, I feel someone standing behind me, massaging my neck. One might think that, as a homie once said to me, it's a "fragment of my imagination." But I know, like one knows such things, it is my father, even though he's been dead for ten years. I feel thumbs digging into the sinews of my neck, right into the area most affected by these old fear-filled storylines. And I'll be damned: Fitch shampoo and Aqua Velva. I cry, as only one can after having been massaged into a newfound sense of sacred presence, deepened peace, and an unshakable holy assurance.

We think that holiness has a particular look. I once saw an ad for a play about the Polish mystic Faustina, the messenger of Divine Mercy. The actress was encased in a black habit, eyes gazing upward, looking gentle, meek, and mild. A saint, portrayed as you'd expect: soft-spoken, even a tad mousy, humorless, and ill at ease, I suppose, with anything less than tidy. Sainthood, and therefore holiness, has been presented in an inaccessible, antiseptic way. "Saintliness" has become a far cry from "sainthood." One can't help but think of the *New Yorker* cartoon in which a man stands at the pearly gates before Saint Peter, who is seated at a desk, peering at a computer. Peter says to the guy, "You say 'meek,' but our records show 'passive-aggressive.'" We settle for the look of holiness rather than the likes of it.

Holy does not look like Mando. Late one night, I'm riding my bike in the Pico Gardens Housing Projects, struck by how deserted it seems to be. Then I spot Mando, a sixteen-year-old gang member, sitting alone on the stoop of his apartment. Kindness was this kid's hallmark. Once I was talking to him on the phone and found his manner so compellingly gentle that I said, "Mando, it's a privilege to be speaking with you."

"You?" he replied in genuine surprise. "*Me*! I'm on one knee."

This particular evening I roll up on him, straddling my dark-blue beach cruiser, and ask, "What are you doing out here?"

"Praying," he says, matter-of-factly. "In fact," he continues, "I asked God just now to give me a sign that He's as great as I think He is. Then you showed up. Proof!"

It's the holiest person, I would assert, who is on the lookout for such moments of spaciousness and calm. Like Mando, sitting on his porch, finding his heart once again restored to some beauty, innocence, and wholeness. The Sufis call this hearing "the voice of the Beloved." I've given up trying to be as holy as Mando, though I do have the desire for the desire. Print a holy card with his mug on it.

I was invited to speak in San Francisco at a luncheon at the Ritz-Carlton titled Unsung Heroes of Compassion, with the opening keynote delivered by His Holiness the Dalai Lama. We were instructed by the Secret Service not to stand when he entered the large ballroom, so we remained seated, the only sound coming from a violinist playing onstage, as His Holiness snaked through the room and stopped to chat with a teenage boy with an aggressive cancer, whose last wish was to meet him. They interacted for a bit, the crowd still hushed in reverence, and then he climbed the steps to the stage. The music faded out. As he made his way to a huge easy chair in the center of the platform, a sound guy hurriedly placed one of those Madonna microphone headpieces around his ear. When he planted himself on the cushions, he let out a relieved, growling, "Oh, *yeah*." The crowd laughed, in a shared, human recognition that comes from rest after a long, rambling walk. He spoke at the beginning, and I gave the closing address. It was quite something to have the Dalai Lama seated in a chair to my left as I spoke, listening and even laughing. (Isn't that on everybody's bucket list? Visit Machu Picchu. Check. Make the Dalai Lama laugh. Check.)

Shortly afterward, a friend sent me a YouTube video clip of His

Holiness at another event, being interviewed by a man and a woman sitting on a couch who ask him about the holy and the sacred. They lean in, anticipating his answer. He proceeds to share with them the joys and sanctity of passing gas. He is beside himself giggling, wildly amused by his choice of topic, and also at the apoplectic response of his interviewers. He even goes so far as to demonstrate how to relieve one's gas pressure on a plane ride. He can barely speak, he's laughing so hard, leaning and raising a holy cheek to illustrate. The two on the couch are all but hiding under the cushions. Hafez wrote:

> *Slipping on my shoes,*
> *boiling water,*
> *toasting bread,*
> *buttering the sky,*
> *That should be enough contact*
> *With God in one day*
> *To make everyone "crazy."*

Oh, and did I mention passing gas?

Every single moment of our lives asks us to be charmed, captivated, enticed, thrilled, and pleased. We don't wait for such moments to fall out of the sky; we just put ourselves on high alert to catch these moments as they happen. After all, like certain bodily functions, discovering the holy in all things is indeed a process. It is also an impulse, like smiling, which does not await the arrival of joy but actually precedes and hastens it. Being alert to the sacred in our midst is a choice that gets more meaningful as we practice it. My friend Pema Chödrön counsels us to "always maintain a joyful mind." Turns out, joy comes with a "maintenance contract."

At Homeboy there's a big strapping guy by the name of Isma, whose goofiness is contagious. He has a shaved head and tattoos everywhere, with the letter *G* prominently covering the front part of his scalp. One of my sisters met him once and was convinced that the *G* stood for my name. "I love your brother so much," Isma told her, pointing to the tattoo, "I put this on my head." She lectured him, only to find out later that the letter actually stood for the name of his gang.

In addition to yanking chains, Isma is known for creating one of the most cherished practices at Homeboy. Each day, we hold the morning meeting. The reception area and stairwell are packed with hundreds of staff and trainees, plus many hopeful *vatos* waiting to be brought in. Announcements are made, the mission statement is read, the thought for the day is delivered, and the daily calendar is explained. There's also a great deal of interaction. For example, I always turn to the tattoo removal staff and say, "Tattoo removal?" to ascertain the hours the doctors will be here.

Curtis, a gentle-souled African American gang member who works in the tattoo removal clinic—an amputee on crutches—bellows, "All day," and the crowd roars in response, "All. Damn. Day!"

When the coach of our Homeboy basketball team announces that we've lost the previous night's game, the room explodes in the kind of elation normally reserved for a championship win. As the designated Homegirl staffer announces the soup of the day, she concludes, "And with that being said"—they always use this phraseology—"have a nice day." The crowd erupts like someone has announced the birth of a baby. Whoever is leading our closing prayer always begins with "Everyone, bow your heads" and the entire room follows his instructions.

To these beloved routines, Isma has contributed another. Early on, when a trainee would be summoned to read the mission statement or the list of the day's classes, and Isma sensed that they might be nervous, he'd yell out, "I know that guy!" Everyone would laugh, putting the reader at ease. He doesn't do this for everyone or reserve it just for his friends. He shouts it only when he feels someone could really use it. Now others do it as well.

One day Isma is pulled in to be a runner, whose job is to monitor and escort whoever comes into my office to see me. He has "the list" with the names of homies, donors, elected officials, or students who are waiting to speak with me. It's first come, first served, and when I'm done speaking with one homie, I signal to my runner to bring the next one in; one reporter called it "The Godfather will see you now" moment. Isma is thrilled to have the job today. He bounces as he stands there, beaming, with the sacred list, his usual liveliness tenfold. From my glass-enclosed office, I signal him to send in the next person. Instead of tapping the next homie to enter, he stands in my open doorway, arms at his side, and bows. It's like he's the butler from *Downton Abbey*. The only thing missing is him calling me "Your Lordship."

"Your three o'clock appointment is here to see you," he says in a formal tone. I thank him and then watch him turn to a homie standing nearby. "I've always wanted to say that!" he exclaims, his arms flailing like those gangly plastic hot-air guys announcing the grand opening of a strip mall. He can't contain his enthusiasm. Life and the living of the gospel, the entrance into kinship, are supposed to look like this. Isma has learned how to savor the delight rather than wait for it to show up, to be constantly on the lookout for the holy in each moment. Buttering the sky.

A homie named Lencho, his lady, and their two kids are finally able to have their own place. It's not much, but it's theirs. They no longer have to sleep in some in-law's living room or battle for the bathroom. "My life has become so repetitious," he told me once, heavy with sadness. Prison, rehab, addiction, repeat; Lencho had grown weary of it all. He asked me to swing by one day and bless his new home. When I do, I see that the place is sparse, and what they do have has been cobbled together from the furniture donations that find their way to Homeboy. We do the blessing, the two little ones gingerly holding the plastic salad bowl with the holy water as we walk from room to room, spritzing each one. We bless the bathroom *"para que todo salga bien." So that everything comes out okay.* The kids giggle. Afterward, Lencho walks me to my car. "Imagine, G. Our own place. I mean, we can walk around naked!" Lencho found exuberance and wholeness and wasn't going to let this delight pass without savoring it.

A volunteer at the old East Max County Jail stands at the entrance to the mess hall holding a small bowl of holy water. Mass is about to begin and each inmate files in, dips his finger in the water, and makes the sign of the cross. Then I see this one large, bald gang member, after signing himself, dip another finger and lift it carefully, trying to keep the droplet balanced on his fingertip. With his other hand, he deftly removes a photograph from the front of his pants. It was a sonogram, blackish with white swirls. Standing there, holding up the line, he reverently let the drop of holy water fall over the image, making the sign of the cross on it. Then he gently returned the treasured "flika" to his pocket for safekeeping. He saw me, shook my hand and said, "I don't know if it's a boy or a girl—all I know for sure is that it's a blessing."

Saint Ignatius wants us to consider "how God dwells" in things, inviting us to sheer wonder at sonograms and sunsets and everything in between.

I remember a payday at Homeboy Industries, hearing two homies discuss what they'd do with their money. One of them, receiving his first-ever paycheck, said, "I'm gonna take my mom to dinner."

"Hey, fool," his companion replied. "Go to that place Charlie Brown's. They got cloth napkins there." In Bethlehem, the words are printed in stone on the ground: "And the word became flesh . . . here." In the dust, the sweat, the tiny thing, in the cloth napkin and in the last place you'd be looking, it manifests for all to see. The great discovery awaits us in the tiny thing.

I'm always moved by how tender the homies can be with their ladies. Clearly, because they have few touchstones in this regard and have often witnessed fathers or male figures beat down their moms, there is a degree of difficulty for the homies in finding the right tenor of tenderness in relationships with women. I find myself, more often than not, just trying to get couples to fight fair. A homie, Sammy, once came into my office during his shift.

"I gotta go home, G," he said breathlessly. "I gotta get outta here *now*." I try to get him to relax and explain. After a moment he tells me that he and his lady, Erika, have had a bad argument. She thinks that he's been cheating on her. Then he lets me listen to a voice mail message from her: "*Oye, cabrón*. Watcha. I'm about to flush your mom's ashes down the toilet." There's an attention-getter for you. Most days, just fighting fair is victory enough.

Another couple, Shorty and Abby, are in my office on their ten-year anniversary—a lifetime in homie relationships. I ask them how they'll be celebrating.

"I don't know," Shorty says, pulling his lady in, placing his arm around her, and squeezing. "I'm thinking of takin' her ass to Burger King. You know, get her one of them crowns." There is great dissolving of laughter all around, sacred to behold. And being alert to the sacred in our midst is a choice that gets more sure as we practice it.

By the time I got back from being on the road and visited Gonzo at County General Hospital, his right leg had already been amputated below the knee. A week earlier he had been standing in front of a house, at a baptismal party, when a car pulled up. Someone inside opened fire and leveled Gonzo to the ground. The medical team struggled for five days to save the leg before finally giving up.

In the weeks following the shooting, I visited Gonzo almost daily. The doctors told him that in order to be discharged, he had to walk, eat, and pass gas. One day, as I walked into his room, I was greeted with a smile, and exciting news: "G . . . I farted!" I congratulated him and said I'd see to it that his certificate got framed. There was a tear in my eye but a twinkle in his. I had known this guy, now in his late twenties, for most of his life, and somehow, despite the tragedy that had befallen him, it was abundantly clear that he did not want me to walk a path of grief or despair. He tries to steer me in another direction.

"Well, G, I'll never dance again," he said.

"Dog, I've seen you dance," I told him. "You couldn't dance before."

We laugh, but even so, Gonzo wanted to seal the deal and cement some truth while laid out in this hospital bed.

"G, I'm not my leg."

Holy befold.

Our mistakes are not the measure of who we are. Neither are our legs. So we choose to let the right things define us. The Buddhist master can explain his equanimity, peace, and joy by holding up a glass and declaring: "I know this glass is already broken." And Gonzo, a gang member from Boyle Heights, has the light grasp of a saint, freed from the attachments that encase our suffering. He has a taste of what it's like not to be destroyed and liberated from all clinging and fear.

One day, I am in the iconic Sears building in Boyle Heights to get my supply of gift cards for returning citizens. I hear a "Hey, G!" and turn to see this tiny fellow, Mario, wearing a Sears work shirt and towing a metal rack filled . . . with the largest bras I have ever seen. They fill the length of the iron rod, D cups—and even higher on the alphabet—suspended on hangers. Mario is a small but stocky man covered in tattoos. He's wearing one of those Velcro back braces as a precaution. These are some heavy brassieres.

"It's great to see you, G," he says loudly, causing some shoppers to turn their heads. I ask him how he got a job at the store. "Your people found it for me," he explains. Then he speaks a bit of the life he had lived before and in his voice there is a trace of regret for time lost. "That's it for me, G. No more shenanigans."

All initiation stories are accounts of journeys involving scaling impossible mountains, going head-to-head with dragons, crossing raging waters. It is the holy and wholly brave risking of the life you know and the welcoming of something entirely new . . . and shenanigan-free.

Mario is exuberant with his new life and childlike in his glee. After lavishing him with my pride and affirmation, there is a pause, and I suppose my eyes darted to the merchandise he is hauling. His eyes go there too. "Imagine, G," he says, loud and beaming. "They got my ass on bras!"

———————

Everyone has shorthand with their friends, those cut-to-the-chase expressions that indicate larger ideas that come from the mundane and ordinary. I'm on a train with my friend Mark, a Jesuit and Homeboy coworker. A very large man comes ambling down the aisle. He already appears to be a number of sheets to the wind and is headed to the train's bar, hoping to add a few more. But when he gets to our row, he stops. He stares straight ahead and then belches so loudly, it produces gasps from the other passengers. It's the burp heard round the world. Couples are muttering, "Why I never in my *life*," disgusted, beside themselves with horror. The man then continues toward his destination. Mark turns to me and smiles.

"Life's great," he says.

That's been our shorthand ever since. If some hiccup of unpleasantness finds its way into one of our routines, we'll share it with each other, pause, and say, sometimes in unison: "Life's great." How, then, do we, as Hafez suggests, "stay close to any sounds that make you glad you are alive." And why would we put a limit on such sounds? This is not so far from Ignatius' call to find God in all things.

My favorite "Life's great" story of Mark's (and I don't know anyone who has more of them) happened when he was very young on a Halloween night. He was going house to house with his buddies, dressed like a ghost, two eyeholes in a sheet. They arrived at a door, and Mark, per usual, was the very last to get to the woman doling out goodies, the Charlie Brown of trick-or-treaters. When he finally got to the front of the line, she said that she'd run out of candy. Suddenly she exclaimed, "Oh, wait! Titi's tu-tus." She returned and dropped something in Mark's bag. She closed the door just as a dog began to bark from inside the house. "Titi, hush!" he could hear her say. When he went through his loot at home later that night, he discovered, in his bag, among his candy, two very firm turds, belonging, presumably, to Titi.

"Wouldn't you know it," Mark says. "My friends get the good crap, and I get, well, crap."

Then we say, like some antiphonal refrain: "Life's great."

Not only is this story better than a Reese's Peanut Butter Cup, it's right and true. On occasion, some deranged woman is going to drop some turds in your bag. No one is asking you to eat them. You marvel at such a thing, recognizing that life can often be more curious than not. And, well, yes, . . . life's great. Wisdom reminds us, "Your imperishable spirit is in all things."

Back when the original Homeboy bakery was across the street from Dolores Mission Church, before it burned to the ground in October 1999, I paid one of my evening visits around closing time. Forced to park some distance from the bakery, I can see the building's lone light by the entrance. I'm distracted by three teenage girls. Their fingers are lightly gripping the chain-link fence facing the parking lot and the front door of the bakery, and they are giggling uncontrollably. I can hear the blaring sound of cumbia music. Then I see the source of their amusement. Big old Danny, one of our bakers, is dancing a raucous cumbia with tiny Carlitos, another baker, both from rival gangs, arm in arm, in their white bakery uniforms, covered in flour, swirling each other to these girls' endless delight.

C. S. Lewis wrote that "holiness . . . is irresistible." It is our inkling, naturally, to suspect that doing tiny, decent things possesses a great power. It is a world-altering holiness in which our truest selves long to participate. I once walked into the restroom at Homeboy and noticed that two stalls were occupied. Suddenly someone spoke: while they were doing their business, one homie was doling out marital advice to the guy in the adjacent stall. "She just needs you to listen to her. Talk less. Open your ears more. Watch what happens, dog."

And with that being said . . . life's great.

———

At the turn of the century, I am diagnosed with leukemia and rushed into chemotherapy. I tolerate it all reasonably well. I tell a friend that, on any given day during chemo, however, I feel like one or more of the Seven Dwarfs. I may be Grumpy, Dopey, or Sleepy. Occasionally, I'll even be one of their cousins, Gassy, Poopy, or Queasy. In the midst of my treatments, I get a call that Bird has been in a very serious car accident.

Bird, now in his twenties, was one of the most truly knuckleheaded gang members I have ever known. For a long time he was impervious to all offers of help. He loved smoking cools (PCP), shooting at enemies, and being provocative at every turn. I always gave him lots of credit for a goodly portion of my white hair. I did get him a job early on, but he got shot and never returned to work. Though fully recovered, he'd thrown in the towel.

But the last couple of years, Bird has turned things around, working and becoming a dedicated husband and father of two. Recovery has become part of the air he breathes. I have often seen him at Homeboy, where he regularly attends NA meetings. "We've been on the battlefield together, G," he says during one of his visits. Indeed, we have.

Now, in between chemo sessions, I slip over to the ICU at

General Hospital to visit him. Even before the cancer, I was not a stranger to hospital horrors. Nothing surprises or startles me much anymore, having seen human bodies rearranged every which way, but seeing Bird takes my breath away. Virtually every bone in his body is broken. Both his legs are suspended and in casts, held together by an amazing array of pins. He is immobile and intubated, unable to speak, with IVs everywhere. I've never seen a body so devastated and dismantled as the one lying before me. His eyes look startled when he sees me. They bloom and come alive. There is no panic in them, only a steady sense, the ground of all being. His gaze locks onto mine. My eyes glisten.

I go on and on about how he'll make it, how much we all love him, etc. The things you say. I just keep talking, trying to derail the discomfort and anguish that so fill me as I stand there at his bedside. I ask to say a prayer over him, and I do so, placing my hand on his forehead and anointing him with oil used for the Sacrament of the Sick. When I'm done, he gestures barely with his right hand, indicating his desire to write something. A few of the fingers in his right hand seem to be the only operative bones in this man's body. I grab a small pad of paper on a nearby table and hand him my pen.

After much labor, Bird writes this: "But YOU, G? How are YOU doing?" Both "yous" are capitalized. I begin to cry. I hold my face in my hands, powerless in the presence of such soaring generosity.

Suddenly the alarm on a machine goes off. I ask what it means.

"I'm going to self-destruct," he writes. Then he makes "blowing up" gestures as best he can, rescuing me, I suppose, from this overwhelming, emotional fullness in which I find myself.

As I leave, I say, "All I know is, I sure love you a lot, Philip," I say, using his given name.

He makes one last panicky wave for pen and paper. "I love you MORE," he writes.

Barking to the Choir

The divine always wants to be liberated, no longer confined for too long in compartments so tiny. That holy amazement at God wants to burst forth, to blossom and bloom, and to be made flesh . . . here. Since the glass is already broken, might as well make as much contact with God to make us all crazy.

CHAPTER THREE

"And Awe Came upon Everyone"

Lately I've been taking a leisurely stroll through the Acts of the Apostles. This section of the New Testament is not only a quaint snapshot of life in the earliest Christian community but also a lesson in how to measure the health in any community at all. When you read Acts through this lens, things start to leap off the page. "See how they love one another." Not a bad gauge of health. "There was no needy person among them." A better metric would be hard to find.

There is one line that stopped me in my tracks: "And awe came upon everyone." It would seem that, quite possibly, the ultimate measure of health in any community might well reside in our ability to stand in awe at what folks have to carry rather than in judgment at how they carry it.

Homies often say, "I was raised on the streets," but Monica truly was. Homeless, a gang member, and a survivor, her behavior at Homeboy can often be alarming. She once kicked in our glass front door. On another particularly wild rampage, she went into our kitchen and began to gulp down a purple all-purpose cleaner call Fabuloso. ("Fabulosa" later became her nickname among the homies.)

Despite these outbursts, I still hope she'll get caught up in the rapture of the Holy Trinity—Recovery, Meds, and Therapy—but you take victories where you can. I once corrected her for speaking with some harshness to one of the trainees.

"But that's why I told her to 'Shut up,'" she said, stone-faced, "instead of 'Shut up, you fucking bitch.'" Progress. Awe compels us to try and understand what language her behavior is speaking. Judgment never gets past the behavior.

After another incident, Father Mark tells her, with tenderness, "I wish I could adopt you."

"You would not want me for a daughter," she tearfully replies.

"Course I would," he says. "It would never be boring."

Mark knows he can't carry what Monica carries. But he can carry her.

Once I was invited to speak to six hundred social workers in Richmond, Virginia. Often I'll say yes to invitations like these without studying the details too carefully. I assumed the Richmond event was some keynote or lunchtime address, but when I later read the not-so-fine print, I realized that I had committed myself to a daylong in-service on gangs, from 9:00 a.m. to 5:00 p.m.—and I was to be the only speaker. I made this discovery a week before I was to fly. So I invited two trainees into my office, DeAndre and Sergio. "Look, you're flyin' with me to Richmond, Virginia," I tell them. "I want you to get up and tell your stories. Take your time . . . cuz we got a long-ass day to fill."

Sergio was in his mid-twenties, a tattooed gang member who

had served considerable time in prison. He also had been homeless for a stretch and an active heroin addict for a longer one. I knew patches of his backstory: drinking and sniffing glue at eight, which eventually led to crack, PCP, and finally heroin. He had been first arrested at nine for assault and breaking and entering, jumped into a gang at twelve, and did two and a half years for stabbing his mom's boyfriend, who tried to abuse him. Sergio began at Homeboy in what we call "the humble place"—the janitorial crew—but in time he became a valued member of our substance abuse team, now solid in his own recovery and helping younger homies try sobriety on for size.

As he stood before the audience in Richmond, Sergio began his story in an offhanded way. "I guess you could say my mom and me, well, we didn't get along so good. I think I was six when she looked at me and said, 'Why don'tcha just kill yourself? You're such a burden to me.'"

Six hundred social workers gasped in unison. Sergio fanned his hands like he was trying to put out a fire. "It sounds way worser in Spanish," he said reassuringly. Everyone laughed. We all got whiplash moving from gasp to laugh. He's one sentence into his story and we all need a laugh.

"I think I was, like, nine years old," Sergio continued, "when she drove me to the deepest part of Baja California, walked me up to the door of this orphanage and said, 'I found this kid.'" He paused, his voice beginning to quietly buckle. "I was there ninety days before my grandmother could get out of my mom where she had dumped me, and my grandmother came and rescued me."

He searched for what to say next. "My mom beat me every single day of my elementary school years, with things you could imagine and a lotta things you couldn't. Every day my back was bloodied and scarred. In fact, I had to wear three T-shirts to school each day. The first one cuz the blood would seep through. The second cuz you could still see it. Finally, with the third T-shirt, you couldn't see no blood. Kids at school would make fun of me. 'Hey, fool . . . It's a hundred degrees . . . Why ya wearin' three T-shirts?'"

He paused again so his emotions could catch up to him, momentarily knocking the wind out of his speech. For a time he seemed to be staring at a piece of his story that only he could see.

"I wore three T-shirts," he finally said, swallowing back his tears, "well into my adult years, cuz I was ashamed of my wounds. I didn't want no one to see 'em." Then he suddenly found a higher perch upon which to rest. "But now I welcome my wounds. I run my fingers over my scars. My wounds are my friends.

"After all," he continued, barely getting out the words, "how can I help others to heal if I don't welcome my own wounds?"

And awe came upon everyone.

The fourteenth-century mystic Dame Julian of Norwich thought that the truest and most authentic spiritual life was one that produced awe, humility, and love. But awe gets lost in that triad. We are at our healthiest when we are most situated in awe, and at our least healthy when we engage in judgment. Judgment creates the distance that moves us away from each other. Judgment keeps us in the competitive game and is always self-aggrandizing. Standing at the margins with the broken reminds us not of our own superiority but of our own brokenness. Awe is the great leveler. The embrace of our own suffering helps us to land on a spiritual intimacy with ourselves and others. For if we don't welcome our own wounds, we will be tempted to despise the wounded.

Henry, who I've known for some time, was languishing in East LA Doctors Hospital after an appendectomy. Put a homie in a hospital and he becomes the child he may or may not have been. Henry had been fatherless, and though his mother was there, it was a rudderless connection. "I guess I just got the wrong mom," he told me once. He was eighteen and had already settled for the dark and shallow life of gang existence. That toughness, however, faded quickly once he was put into a hospital gown and hooked up to machines.

"Does it hurt?" I asked him when I visited.

"Only when I breathe," he quietly admitted. I encouraged him not to breathe, then. But he was in no laughing mood.

I asked him what he longed for and looked forward to.

"You mean what do I want to be when I grow up?" he said, and sneered. But then the air of smart-ass disappeared and suddenly he was left in a desolate, sad place. "Oh, G, I gave up a long-ass time ago, thinking 'bout my future." He seemed startled by a tear's appearance. "Yup, there's nuthin' there. Nuthin' there."

Often what is discovered in the wings of pain is a shame to which folks cling. After work one day, I have a conversation in my office with Alex, an older *vato* who is starting to allow memories from his youth to rise to the surface. He is nine years old and his parents are fighting behind the locked door of their bedroom. There are not just screams and shouting, he explains, but noises suggesting flying *cuerpos* and furniture upheaval. Alex is outside pounding on the door, tears streaming down his face, yelling desperately, "Stop! Please, stop!"

Then, with all his power and strength, this little kid kicks that door down—as much to his surprise as anyone else's. It flops right off its hinges, wood splinters flying, landing in the room and falling on the bed. His parents are stunned and they stare at their child. All three are silent. Soon the father clutches his face in his hands and sobs without reserve.

"Then my dad ran past me and out of the room," Alex remembers. "Out of the house, and out of our lives, forever." He cries now, much the same, I imagine, as his father had those many years ago. "And it's all my fault." What is most crushing sometimes is not the pain, exactly, but what stands right behind it—"Not what happens to us in childhood," poet Jack Gilbert writes, "but what was inside what happened."

Jorge is truly shaken, sobbing uncontrollably in front of me. He doesn't waste any time in telling me why. He's come from his home, where he held his mom and his lady at gunpoint.

"I'm twenty-three years old and I'm already tired," he says. "I want to sleep and not wake up." He cries all the more. "My parents beat me and I always cried, until I decided that they'd never make me cry again. They beat me and beat me, but I never cried again." When an even greater clarity grips him, he says, "I don't want to belong to my wounds." Mary Oliver writes, "Let everyone in the world who suffers, have a day off."

We spend so much time asking where our suffering comes from, it leaves us little time to ask where it leads. In the high-poverty urban communities of Los Angeles County, one in three youth suffers from post-traumatic stress disorder. That's twice the rate of soldiers returning from war. Every single homie who walks through our doors brings with him or her a storehouse of unspeakable acts perpetrated against them, from torture, abuse, and violence to abandonment, neglect, and terror. When homies are finally ready and able to tell their stories, they can claim that pain and take control of it. It would be hard to overstate the courage this requires or the time this kind of journey takes. A homie said to me once, "We got authenticity beaten out of us." As they tell their own version of things, for perhaps the first time, they can truly begin to hear it. The moment one says, "This is what it was like for me," a rebirth occurs. Locating our wounds leads us to the gracious place of fragility, the contact point with another human being. When we share these shards of excavation with each other, we move into the intimacy of mutual healing. Awe softens us for the tender glance of God, then enables us to glance in just the same way.

We must try and learn to drop the burden of our own judgments, reconciling that what the mind wants to separate, the heart should bring together. Dropping this enormous inner burden of judgment allows us to make of ourselves what God wants the world to ultimately be: people who stand in awe. Judgment, after all, takes up the room you need for loving.

Readying oneself for awe, at every turn, insists that compassion is always the answer to the question before us. A homie once told me something that had happened to him when he was seven. Some thirty years removed from it, he felt he could now safely return to this scene without fear. His mother and father had been screaming ferociously at each other, and the fight reached a crescendo when the father, with a certain calm and a single punch, decked the mother out cold. As she lay there on the floor, unconscious, his father turned to him and said, "Now, *that's* how you hit a woman."

The story is horrifying. But with that horror comes a compulsion to turn away in judgment, especially of the father, who was almost certainly mentally ill or had been exposed to a similar violence as a kid himself. In moving away from the father, we in turn move away from the son, whose eventual gang activity we will abhor, but who was surely shaped by such a moment and could have used our empathy the most to prevent the cycle from continuing. Kinship asks us to move from blame to understanding. Our practice of awe empties a room, and suddenly there is space for expansive compassion. "Walk in my presence," God says to Abraham, "and be without blame."

At Homeboy, we've discovered through the stories we've heard that trauma can be as much about biology as it is about pathology. In response, we try to create a community rooted in resilience. When Rascal came home after four years in the California Youth Authority, his mom threw him a simultaneous "Welcome Home" and "Farewell" party, which I attended. She explained the dual approach to those of us gathered in the backyard. "You haven't seen him for a while, and now you won't see him again for a while," she said matter-of-factly. Instead of solely celebrating her son's return, she was already assuming that he would soon return to his old ways. Rascal indeed went back to prison, but one wonders if the outcome wouldn't have been different if only one banner had been hanging at his party.

A homie named Saul nearly overdoses on heroin. His ten-year-old son Louie writes him a letter, delivering it to his hospital room. Today, Saul has the letter, exactly as written, handwriting and all, tattooed on his calf.

"I suppose I could have just saved the letter," he told me once. "But I wanted it on me so I could read it every day."

Dear Dad:

I don't have much to say but I want you to stop doing drugs. I don't want you to die at a young age. I want you to be there when I have a child. It was a sad moment when my Mom told me what happened to you. Well, that's all I wanted to say.

PS: Please stop.

Sincerely,
Your 1st son.
I love you.

———

Over a decade ago, I did something of a disappearing act while undergoing chemotherapy for leukemia. When my birthday rolled around, the people insisted that I leave my seclusion, celebrate the Eucharist, and party with them at Dolores Mission. Unsurprisingly, the experience was overwhelming. I could barely get through the mass, pausing often to find my composure. The church was filled with song, and the amazing spirit of the people, where I had been pastor for six years, left me reeling. My soul returned to myself, feeling its worth.

After mass, the crowd ushered me out to the plaza, where one of the usual feasts awaited us. A short woman approached and hugged me. I reached down and kissed her on her forehead.

"And Awe Came upon Everyone"

"So you know?" she asked. I said yes, thinking this woman was Lupe Montes, whose eldest daughter, I'd heard, in her seventh month of pregnancy had just given birth to a stillborn boy. But as I continued to hold her, I realized that this was not Lupe Montes. Wrong Lupe. And yet I could have hugged and kissed anyone in the courtyard that evening, all poor and laden with burdens—way more than most—and any one of them could have asked, "So you know what I'm carrying?"

A homie called me on the phone and broke down in tears, lamenting his terminally ill refrigerator. All the food in it had gone bad and he found himself at the very end of a very worn and tattered rope. When he showed up in my office some hours later for help, he apologized for having had, what he called, an "appliance melt-down." Instead of saying this thing had been the "straw that broke the camel's back," he said, "And that's what got the camel to fall."

It is a self-help maxim of the privileged to say, "Don't sweat the small stuff." But the folks at the bottom have to. What the privileged consider "small stuff" are precisely the trips and traps that foil the folks at the bottom: no bank account; no car, or one that can reliably get you where you're going; no health insurance; several dollars short of a package of Pampers (and when you have a poopy baby and no diapers, I'd say "sweating" would indeed be in order). It isn't simply that being poor means having less money than the privileged; it's that being poor means living in a continual state of acute crisis. This is what they have to lug around every day.

The poor are always one straw away from calamity and catastrophe. Homies who have now chosen to "play by the rules" often find themselves stuck in what I call the "forced-choice economy," having to choose between, say, feeding their kids or paying their rent. Doing without heat and electricity or putting gas in the car. There is a good chance that the camel will fall for them today. Living in such precariousness is stressful. Yet navigating that kind of stress is also awe-inspiring.

Barking to the Choir

A homie named Cruz spent his last dollars taking a Metrolink train sixty miles to Los Angeles from San Bernardino, where he had relocated his lady and newborn to avoid the dangers and desperation of his previous gang life. He had a part-time job but could not get his boss to give him more hours. Now he sits in my office, rattling off a list of the pressures and needs of his family. With no safety net in sight but me, he speaks of no food in the fridge, no lights, landlord looming, no bus fare. When he finishes this breathless account, Cruz stops, shaken and exhausted. He grows teary-eyed and says quietly, "I just keep waiting."

"For what, son?" I ask.

"For the last to be first."

On the mountain tonight the full moon
faces the full sun. Now could be the moment
when we fall apart or we become whole.
Our time seems to be up—I think I even hear it stopping.
Then why have we kept up the singing for so long?
Because that's the sort of determined creature we are.
Before us, our first task is to astonish,
And then, harder by far, to be astonished.

—Galway Kinnell

Deciding to be determined and finally astonished. When judgment ceases to consume all the oxygen in the room, an astonishing love takes its place and we can then be touched by it all.

A homie explained to me: "It's like looking through a window. It's rainy and stormy. The wind's blowing. You see it, but it's not touchin' you." In order to truly understand, you must open the window and try to touch the rain for yourself.

At Camp Paige, a young man named Efrain is about to make

his First Communion. The volunteers rustled up a starched white shirt and a thin black tie for him to wear with his county-issue jeans. He was nervous as he waited for his mom and brother to arrive, and so was I. Many a time a homie has waited for parents who have promised they'll be there, only to be plummeted into disappointment, and I fear the same is about to happen to Efrain. It'll be hard to wait much longer and delay the start of mass, I think to myself, when his mom suddenly arrives, holding the hand of a young man. It turns out this is Efrain's older brother, who is clearly autistic and struggling to acquaint himself with this strange place. They get settled, mass begins, and Efrain beams. We are not too long into the service, however, when his brother has a meltdown, the likes of which, really, no one has ever seen. It is so full-force—screaming and kicking and the flailing of arms and legs—that it takes all of Efrain's physical and emotional power to escort his brother outside. Through the gym doors, I could see his mother calmly sit down with him on a bench, waiting for the fit to pass, but the screaming continues, unabated. Efrain, granite-faced and solemn, makes his First Communion. His mom and brother witness none of it.

Afterward, when I approached Efrain to check in on him, I expected rage, a heaping of blame and frustration that his day had been ruined because of his brother. Instead, Efrain starts to gently sob as he points to his brother, who is methodically rocking back and forth on the bench.

"He has never sinned," he says, trying to gather himself so he can continue. "He is closer to God than any of us."

His mother, close by, hears him and adds in Spanish, "He is the blessing of our lives. We thank God for him every day." Efrain nods in agreement.

I'm at Dolores Mission Church, saying the Sunday evening mass. I've just finished my homily and we are in the midst of the petitionary prayers when I hear from just outside the front doors of the church: "Fuck you, fuck you. I will *not* shut up."

From where I stand, I can't see who the "fuckmeister" is, though I can tell it's a female voice. Lots of heads are turning, and some "cheerleaders" (a homie expression for folks who jump in the mix) head for the door, wanting, I suppose, to squash the disruption. There is another moment of silence during the petitions, and then the yelling turns to screaming at all decibel levels. I finally recognize the voice. It belongs to Crazy Shopping Cart Lady Lucy (as the homies call her).

"Father Greg knows what I'm saying!" I hear her scream. I finish the petitionary prayers, walk to the choir, and tell them in Spanish to sing the offertory hymn: "Sing every verse. Twice." I make my way down the side aisle to the back of the church.

Lucy is in her forties, with stringy blond hair, and is in "I don't need meds" mode. Her face is red from anger and many unprotected days in the sun. Drugs, cigarettes, and life on the streets have leathered her up. She's ranting on and on about how people are "out to kill" her and how someone owes her $300. She takes a breather and for a moment it is a welcome silence. Then she sighs. "You try pushin' this cart 24/7," she says.

The comment is not meant for me but for the cosmos. I consider the offer, though, and we both nod in silence. Then—and why, I don't know—we both burst out laughing. It is full-throated, and as soon as it happens we remember where we are and try to shush and stifle each other. I give her twenty bucks and, with a hug, we tell each other how much we love the other. Indeed we do. "If you weren't a priest," she says before pausing to look at me, "I would rock your world." We howl even more.

"Lucy," I say, "best offer I've gotten all day." We are still laughing as she wheels away. I reenter the church as the choir is finishing the last verse for the second time.

The "monsters at the margins" are constantly under threat and they breathe in shame with every breath. They understandably think that their only recourse is defense and survival. When we conspire with God to move toward this transcendent awe, we are left with only a gentle touch, a tender laugh, and "survivor brain" gets soothed as never before.

Pablo is thoroughly tattooed, nervous all the time (which leads him to stammer), and easily flummoxed. Make no mistake, though: he's tough. Don't pick a fight with him—he'll beat your ass, but only if backed into a corner. He tries so hard to avoid that corner, a big guy with gentleness to spare. One day he takes another homie's place at the front desk at Homeboy, covering for him while he's at lunch. Suddenly he appears at my office door, frantic.

"Stephanie's here to see you," he says, pointing back to a woman with two kids who is waiting in the reception area. Usually the front desk guy will send a note in via one of our "runners" to tell me "Stephanie is here 2-C-U" scribbled down. But Pablo delivers this message himself. He tells me he doesn't know how to spell "Stephanie."

The next day the tables turn when I'm sent a "Pablo 2-C-U" note. He comes into my office and is as apoplectic as I've ever seen him. "I need Yadira," he says, referring to a homegirl who works here.

"Why?" I ask.

"I won't know how to explain—I'll stutter too much." I assure him that when talking to me he does not need to have his "attorney" present.

Pablo explains that, when he went home for lunch earlier that day, he and his lady, the mother of his three children, had a fight. They bicker about a lot of things, and often. I took them both out for dinner once, for some marriage counseling over burritos. "I wish we were like other couples," Pablo later sighed. "You know, all lovey-dovey."

In my office, I ask him what the fight was about. "There's not enough for this month's rent." I give him the money he needs.

The next day Pablo sidles up to me, puts his arm around me, and hands me a note. He tells me to read it, but later. I turn to him and see that he's crying. When I get home that night, I find his note in my pocket and pull it out to read.

> *To my real Pops. Thank you for helping me and my family. I realy realy appecated the things you do for me and for others. I realy love you Pops. My real Pops don't do this for me. Thank you Pops and Merry C-Max.*

I guess it must have been Christmastime.

Along with delivering a keynote address at a conference in Palm Springs, I've been asked to offer a workshop on mentoring. Always seeking to lessen my workload, I arrive with two homies in tow, Manny and Chubbs. "Tell your stories," I tell them, "and be sure to mention someone who has mentored you in your life."

Manny is a solidly built gang member, his "barrio" etched across his face in every imaginable way—diagonally on his cheek, filling the space of his neck, in Roman numerals on his forehead. His very face invites you to judge him.

He arrived at Homeboy only a handful of months earlier, and this would be his first foray into public speaking. I sit in the back of the cramped conference room, feeling like the man in Gerard Manley Hopkins's poem "Brothers" as his younger brother performs onstage, "His tear-tricked cheeks of flame / For fond love and for shame."

Manny stands in front of the small crowd and describes brief snapshots of his upbringing and family life, with both parents gang-involved and in the clenches of drug use. "I ran away from home at nine—couldn't take it no more," he says, almost casually. "It took my mom one month before she asked this question: 'Hey . . . anybody seen Manny?'"

"And Awe Came upon Everyone"

Eventually he gets to the part about his mentor.

"His name was Rafa and he lived next door to me. I was like six, and he was way older, maybe sixteen or seventeen, in high school already," he explains. "He knew how hard it was in my house, so every day he'd pick me up and make sure I got to school. Every day, he'd rescue me. He'd give me good advices—you know, stuff like 'Stay away from gangs,' 'Stay in school,' 'See those guys over there? Avoid them,' 'Stay on this side of the street,' 'Don't ever go in that alley.' He gave me proper-ass advices. Once he said to me, 'I'm gonna graduate from high school and so will you. I'm gonna go to college and so will you. I'm gonna go to medical school and become a doctor. Then I'm gonna come back and take you with me. You'll be my son."

Manny begins an emotional disintegration that has built slowly but is now rising to full view like floodwaters soaking a carpet from below. "Tear-tricked cheeks of flame."

"Yeah . . . I guess I was six," he goes on. "Rafa came to get me like always. As we walked to school and talked, some guys from across the street, the same ones he always said to avoid, started yelling things like 'Where you from?' and like that. Rafa shines them on, waves his arm, says to me, 'Keep walkin.' We walk faster and faster. But they keep askin', again and again, and Rafa says something like 'I ain't from nowhere.' Suddenly, one of 'em is right by us, standing next to Rafa, askin' the same question. In an instant . . . my face is splattered with blood and little pieces of Rafa's brain—all over my face. Rafa is on the ground . . . gaspin' for air. Them guys left and by the time anyone came to help, Rafa had died."

Manny suspends his story, so he can half collapse in sobbing, without regard for the fifty folks transfixed before him.

"After that," he continues, with a resolve to stay within this story's truth, "I did not talk for a month. For thirty days, I did not utter or speak a single word." Suddenly the entire audience found itself in a place of lavish forgiveness at what the sight of Manny led them to think when they first laid eyes on him. Awe trading places with judgment, swiftly and cleanly, "for fond love and for shame."

Ezekiel tells me that today is his last day with Homeboy. I'm surprised by this and ask him why.

"It's the drug testing," he explains. "I just can't do it anymore, and I'd rather be honest with you." He makes a certain calculation in his mind before proceeding. "I don't know. So much pain, and I guess I'm used to numbing it. Thanks anyway, G."

William Morris Hunt, an American painter who lived in Paris in the late 1800s, was a grouchy, depressive guy. He hated the Eiffel Tower. Someone asked him, "Then why do you spend so much time at the Eiffel Tower?" He says, "It's the only place I can't see it from." Homies are saddled with a boatload of pain. They kick it in their "barrios," because it is the only place they can't see their pain from. Or they get high, also a place from which they can't see or feel their wounds.

They say, in recovery, "it takes what it takes" for people struggling with addiction to turn their lives around. Homeboy Industries is not for those who need help, only for those who want it. A gang member, after all, has to actually walk through our doors.

A homie, released from Youth Authority, is right back in the projects, kicking it with his neighborhood. I confront him.

"I guess I'm just not ready yet," he says. There's more sadness in his voice than heightened posturing.

"*Mijito*," I tell him, "don't wait to be ready. *Decide* to be ready."

Even so, there's no telling what the precipitating event, person, or moment might be that gets a gang member to cross our threshold. It can be the death of a friend, the birth of a son, a long stretch in prison. It takes what it takes.

A homie, packing a gun, walks in front of a church and stops momentarily to *persignarse* (cross himself). An old woman selling *paletas* nearby asks him why he just made the sign of the cross.

"For protection," he answers.

"That's strange," she boldly replies, "cuz, given the terror you bring to this community, we are all asking God to protect us from you."

That conversation was all it took for him to hang up his gloves forever.

Jamal came to Homeboy because a homie of his, Trayvon, had been a trainee and suggested that HBI might welcome him as he himself had been welcomed. But before Jamal could reach us, Trayvon was gunned down at a picnic. Jamal later told me, "That only strengthened my desire to change." The youngest of six kids, he had been born and raised in Indianapolis. His single mother had a job and owned her own home, but soon lost both. They spent that first winter in a shelter and then, come spring, moved to Los Angeles to begin anew. "Things did not work out as we had hoped." Money started dissipating like early-morning fog. Jamal's mom couldn't find work, and so they kept moving around Los Angeles, their apartments getting smaller and smaller, and closer and closer to Skid Row. Soon they were in hotels and, finally, sleeping on the streets themselves.

"One morning," he recounted, "as my mom was packing up our few belongings and the tarp we used for shelter, I watched a bunch of kids waiting to get on a school bus. I wanted, more than anything, to go with them. My mom told me that if I went, she wouldn't be here when I got back. I followed that bus to the school, but apparently you can't just show up at school. You sort of need a parent, and to be enrolled, so I left. When I got back to Skid Row, my family was gone. I looked everywhere. I wandered the streets all night and never found my mom or my family. I realized, that night, I was on my own. I was seven years old."

It took several years for the "system" to find Jamal, and once it did, he began a new life in foster care. By the time he reached high school age, he had been raised by several surrogate parents, who were so abusive that they would wake him up in the middle of the night just to beat him and lock him out of the house for hours on end.

He joined a gang at thirteen and was subsequently kicked out of five schools. He was locked up for two long stints before he was eighteen, and returned to jail again for seven years. It was during that time that he started to rethink things. He started to read books and got his GED.

"In the end, I gave in," he later wrote about the experience. "I gave in to the sadness of all those years of neglect and abandonment. I gave in to the terror I never let myself feel—as I watched people being beaten, thrown out of windows, and killed on Skid Row. I gave in to, I realize, not sadness and fear but anger. I learned the word 'schizophrenia' and came to terms with the fact that my mom did not hurt me on purpose." Today his mother is still alive and lives under a bridge in Los Angeles. "I hope that one day I can help her find her way home."

A homie named Isidro writes to me from jail. "I went on a symbolic hunger strike. I gave up some symbols—like feeling sorry for myself—I just stopped feeding that to myself. And the idea of success. I hate to be called 'a success story.' It implies 'I was this,' now 'I'm that.'"

It's true enough that "everything that counts can't be counted." There is a difference between producing outcomes and chasing them. How do we manage to measure success not in dollars but in change? (I lifted that last sentence from a bank ad.)

A homie who worked for us here and is now employed in a great job elsewhere showed up one day for a visit. "I'm in a happy place now," he said proudly. "It's my day off and I'm here. I love this transformation in me. I love getting up and coming here. It's home."

A kid, just released from YA, whom I had known since he was small, leaves me a voice mail message: "Hey, G, I got mature. Now I just want to be a workaholic. And I don't want ya to give me milk. I want the whole damn cow."

We honor the other and step away from the critique. We seek to embrace what Ignatius called "adoration," which was principally expressed through reverence. We are reverent, then, for the weight carried by those on the margins and stand present before the wordless goodness of our God in them.

With a number of talks scheduled in Philadelphia and Scranton, Pennsylvania, I take Tyrone and Earl to do some of the yakkin'. They are African American gang members who have done prison time, and this is their first plane trip. In the air, I google restaurants in Philadelphia and find the oldest one, supposedly, in the country. Ben Franklin and Betsy Ross apparently double-dated there. I turn to Tyrone to share what I've found.

"Can we have porridge?" he asks earnestly.

The entire adventure defies description for Earl and Tyrone. They excitedly film their hotel room à la MTV's *Cribs*, complete with running commentary. With each talk, they gain confidence and are greeted each time with ovations from the audience, which delights them to no end. High school and college students alike connect with the stories, as both men tell them with poignancy and charm. After the last event, an evening gig packed with folks despite a most impressive rainstorm, Tyrone rushes into the rental car's "shotgun" seat and sighs greatly.

"It's official," he says, smiling. "We're public figures."

The next morning he secures the same seating arrangement as we head to the airport to fly home. Earl, in the backseat, thanks me for these days and an unforgettable trip. Tyrone adds his gratitude.

"It was the best experience of my life." He turns to me and says, "It even beats my *last* best experience." I'm curious and encourage him to elaborate. "Well," he explains, "my last best experience was when I barely got out of prison. My homies threw a welcome home party in a barbershop, with strippers and all the barbecue you can eat." Before I even have time to be startled by this, he leans in quite serious, with emphasis. "This even beats strippers and *all the barbecue you can eat.*"

———

Topo is shirtless and bloody when his older brother, Snoopy, and another homeboy of theirs dump him into the front seat of my car. A big football game at Pecan Park between two gangs has just ended and Topo, well "cooled" by PCP, "took flight" on one of his own homies. The fight, which I was able to see from the other end of the field as it took place, was a rapid-flying slugfest that left Topo down and dazed within seconds of its starting. Still, he doesn't want to leave and so he's hauled, arms draped over the shoulders of his brother and his helper, toward my parked car. "Don't disrespect G" is the repeated admonishment of both as Topo blurts out all manner of expletives. He becomes more draggy and reluctant with every step he takes.

"Take him home for me, G, yeah?" Snoopy asks, already pouring the uncooperative limbs of his sibling into my car. There is an ache in Snoopy's voice as he clicks the seat belt around his kid brother.

I whisk Topo away toward the City of Commerce, where he lives. At first he drifts in and out, but he snaps to attention when we hit the freeway. His shirtless upper torso is marked with mini-streams of blood, grass and dirt stains, and tattoos in all the usual locations. He smells of PCP, Three Flowers hair grease, and cigarettes, and his oversized, cut-off Dickies still retain the fragrance of Ariel blue laundry soap.

"I'm gonna kill him, G," Topo says of the *vato* he has fought. "I'm gonna straight out smoke 'im." He makes his right hand into a gun and shoots at his absent foe. He repeats this refrain and peppers his speech with the words "ranker," "buster," and "*leva*." His rant continues until we get to his house. I pull up, but Topo refuses to budge. "I left my huaraches at the park," he says. "I need to go back for 'em." I tell him that I'll do the retrieving. He needs to go home and sleep things off. "My *jefita* gave me them huaraches. They mean a lot to me. I need to go back and get 'em. 'Sides, you don't even know where they be at." I tell him there are two ways that I will drive him back, as an old Jesuit friend always says: "No way" and "No fucking way."

"Look, *mijo*," I say, "I'm not going to take you back there. We're here. Now just kick back in your house and I'll find your huaraches." Topo tries again to convince me, but after a few attempts, he realizes that I'm not going to budge.

"Okay, then," he says. "I'll just hop on my bike, and pack my *cuete*, and go back to the projects myself. I'll probably shoot a gang a' fools and a bunch a' cops till one of them smokes me." But he doesn't move. We sit in the car for half an hour, the engine running, repeating this madness over and over again.

"I'm not going back to the projects," I tell him again and again. "And I don't want you to disrespect me, *tampoco*, by going back on your own." I begin to repeat the part about feeling disrespected, hoping it'll stick. His response is "Oh, well."

Snoopy soon arrives with his lady, who is eight months pregnant, and other very large homies. He walks alone to my side of the car. He, too, is shirtless, filthy, and sweaty from the football game. The others stand back as Snoopy leans his crossed arms on the driver's door. I place my hand on his shoulder and solicit his help.

"Your *carnal*, *mijo*," I tell him, shaking my head, "is talking a gang a' *masa* and won't even leave my car. I need your *ayudita* here."

Snoopy never takes his eyes off his brother and keeps them locked on him even after I've stopped talking. The words he chooses to say to Topo are slow and deliberate, cracking in his voice before they depart. "Please. Stop. Smoking. That. Shit."

Then Snoopy explodes into wails of the most anguished tears. He rests his head on his folded arms and his body shakes in jerky syncopation with his crying. His homies move to a safe distance from this uncomfortable scene. His lady stays where she is, stroking her large stomach, in gentle rhythm, as if Snoopy were positioned inside.

No more than two brief beats pass before Topo melts into his own crossed arms and wails, in the same language of his brother. There is nothing to do, of course, but to hold each by the nape of his tattooed neck and be the conduit of this immense pain. All their ache and unspeakable sense of loss and abandonment course through my body—from one to the other and back again. In the movement, maybe, the pain subsides, dissipating as it travels. In their lamentation and flood of tears, they speak to each other in a private code, parentless brothers, their own special language of despair, betrayal, and the deepest kind of loneliness.

Without much fanfare, Topo leaves my car and Snoopy word-lessly joins him on the other side. The much-beloved huaraches, it seems, have indeed been retrieved and all is well for these two baby-faced boys who have had to raise themselves and now must enter manhood, lock-armed and in this together.

And this is how they take their leave of me: arms hanging over each other, with half-broken spirits made nearly whole in each other's embrace. Only Snoopy turns his head to me, as they near the house, and mouths a silent "Thank you." I drive back to the projects, steeped in this admixture of certain and privileged grace and palpable dread. How close are these two, I think, to the tender glance of God.

"Now could be the moment when we fall apart or we become whole."

CHAPTER FOUR

Now. Here. This.

You ask the homies on the phone, "What are ya doin'?" and they'll always start off by saying, "Just right here." It probably comes from them translating the Spanish, *"Aquí no más,"* which doesn't exactly work in English. "Just right here, washing my face," a homie might say. "Still got soap on it." "Just right here, watching Jerry Springer." "Just right here, drawing Winnie the Pooh for my daughter." "Just right here, staring at my son."

Jesus would insist that we are saved in the present moment. Just right here. So we choose to practice dwelling in the present moment. We need to find ways to establish ourselves in the here and now. The Buddha teaches that life is only available in the here and now. Jesus doesn't teach differently. We hold out for happiness, healing, transformation, always awaiting a few more conditions that need to be met. This is one of the reasons why happiness eludes us in the now: we still think it's around the corner.

If your anchor is not centered in today, then you'll blink and miss the delight of this very moment, which is always with us and is the perfect teacher. Once, while walking from my Jesuit community to Homeboy's old office, I spotted a ten-year-old I knew named Pepe, who was holding a water-filled plastic bag containing goldfish. There he was, hoisting the bag high, like it was the Olympic torch.

"What ya got there, Peps?" I called out. His speech rarely cooperated with him, the *c*'s and *z*'s and *s*'s coming out of the food processor of his brain and appearing at his mouth misshapen and gnarled.

"Fishishesh!" he yelled, the last letters popping out in a wave of swooshes and spittle. Had I not been across the street at the time, I might have required a toweling down. But Pepe's lift is so high, and so joyous—he's lighting the torch in the stadium—that I nearly cried to myself at the "now" of it.

The discovery that awaits us is that paradise is contained in the here and now. We let go of the desire to expect anything beyond it. The awareness of this keeps us from the suffering generated by resisting life as it is. This ability to stay focused on the present is what some today would call "mindfulness," a kind of attention that can help us all grow rich in the things that matter to God. (According to a recent study, people who practiced mindfulness also were found to have less body fat. I'm still waiting on that outcome.)

A homily I've given in detention facilities (and included in *Tattoos on the Heart*) is a reflection of the scene in which Jesus hangs on the cross between two *ladrones* and then promises one of them, "This day, with me, paradise." There is a seventeen-year-old trainee, straight out of probation camp, named Fabian, who already has his share of adult concerns. With a lady and tiny son, he chooses daily to occupy his own footsteps and steer clear of his past gangbanging pursuits. He remembers this homily and one day delivers it back to me, largely intact.

After a few months of being with Homeboy, Fabian stops in and plunks himself down in my office, telling me he has had a "Paradise sighting." (Later, I distinguish this Fabian from all the others in my cell phone contacts by putting: "Fabian Paradise.")

"Yesterday," he begins, "I was tooken on a ride by God to Paradise."

"Wow," I say to him, "I'm all ears. You had me at 'tooken.'"

"Well, I drove my lady in my tore-up bucket to drop off an assignment at her school. We fought the whole damn time. Petty shit. But we didn't stop. The whole time. She gets out, drops off this thing, gets back in the car, and we fight all the way home. Constant. Nonstop. *Gatos y perros.* Small stuff. Shit that don't matter. Then this noise comes from the hood and smoke starts to pour out. I get off the freeway and pull into this Shell station. My *ranfla* dies as I pull in. I had to push it the rest of the way. I called the *grúa* and it took three hours for the tow truck to arrive." He pauses in his narrative long enough to smile with the tenderness of the memory. "Paradise," he says simply, and nods.

He's lost me here.

"See, G, for three hours we talked. We decided not to fight. We told each other how grateful we are to have each other in our lives. I mean, damn, where would we be if we didn't have each other. We just talked." The smile broadens and gets fixed there.

"Yeah," he says, "Paradise."

Paradise is not a place that awaits our arrival but a present we arrive at. A place, in fact, we are already in. When we expect that moment, we grow more confident that we will be "tooken on a ride" to see it. How many chances a day are we given to recognize this—an opportunity to practice sacred presence? Smack dab, right in front of our eyes. We miss so much "now" because we are rushing to "next."

75

I'm walking with two homies, moving at quite a clip, and outpacing them.

"How come I'm forty years older than you guys and you walk all slow?" I ask.

They both shrug.

"Cuz we're not in a hurry," one says.

Jim Carrey, the comedian and actor, discovered Homeboy Industries by watching the documentary *G-Dog* on Netflix. (He thought it was about actual dogs.) Soon enough, he was visiting our place. He was perfectly present and gracious, somehow recognizing the folks who most needed his attention, and tending immediately to them.

"You're a character, just like me," he said, pointing to Marcos, covered in tattoos. He said the same to Lola as he planted a kiss on her forehead, posing for nonstop selfies and group shots. Kids would stop him during the tour to ask him to do the face from the film *The Mask*, and Carrey would oblige. No request was denied, and none was seen as a bother. I had been nervous and worried that the homies would be over-the-top goofball fans. Suddenly I realized that I was being biblical, and not in a good way. I was being Martha.

In this New Testament passage, Martha is taking all the tasks of hosting Jesus in her home upon herself and then is "butt hurt" that's she's doing everything alone. Her sister, Mary, on the other hand, is sitting at the feet of the rabbi, getting instruction and listening. Jesus commends Mary. What is Mary doing that Jesus likes so much? Mary (and Jim Carrey) have landed on the one thing that is most important: to embrace perfect presence in the moment in front of us.

When I taught at Loyola High School in Los Angeles in the late '70s, after Sunday morning mass I'd grab a cup of coffee and sit in the living room on the second floor and read the *LA Times*. Peace, quiet, and *feliz*; it didn't get better than that. One Sunday, I was sitting with my friend and Jesuit brother, Al Naucke. Both of us had our coffee and were silently turning the pages of the paper when the doorbell started to ring repeatedly. Initially, Al and I hid behind our papers, waiting it out. The doorbell rarely rang, but when it did, it was almost always some homeless person. Finally, Al, the way better man, quietly put down the paper. There was no annoyed sighing (though who would blame him?).

Some ten minutes later he returned, sat down, took a sip of coffee, and resumed his reading. After a few beats I asked, without lowering the paper, "Well?"

"Well what?" Al replied, not lowering his paper either.

"Who was it?"

From behind the sports section he said, "Jesus, in his least recognizable form."

In John's gospel, Mary Magdalene is in a panic at the empty tomb on Easter morning. Weeping, she pleads with a man she thinks is the gardener, "They've taken my Lord, and I don't know where they have lain him." But here's the thing: Mary doesn't know that the gardener is Jesus. His least recognizable form. And so too with the gang member, and the mother receiving welfare, and the heroin addict, and the butcher, the baker, and the candlestick maker. To practice the sacrament of sacred presence is to be Jesus, and to see Jesus. It's all right in front of us, here and now.

In the Spanish-language liturgy at Easter time, there is an opening prayer that looks back to the resurrection of Jesus and then looks forward to what happens to us after death. But there is nothing in the prayer about now. Pema Chödrön invites us to "let ourselves be nailed to the present moment." Certainly, if we live in the past, we will be depressed. If we live in the future, we are guaranteed anxiety. Now is always vast and new. Like any practice, it's not about technique or program. It's a decision.

I ask Gabriel why he is late today. "I got this new soap and it smelled so good, I forgot the time," he says. "'Sides, my kids jumped in the bath." Nailed to the present moment. The "real world" might take exception to this, but it could learn everything from it.

Homies always talk about "doing time" and often refer to something called "dead" time, the period of weeks, months, or years that does not count toward your overall prison sentence. It is the languishing before the clock has been set. And yet, there is no such thing as "dead" time—the moment that doesn't count. All time is alive. Not a second passes that doesn't allow us to ripen, to witness our lives with playfulness, flexibility, and an open heart. Every moment is a chance to wake up and smell that new soap.

Each year at the Dolores Mission parish, a different group—whether it's the kids from the fifth grade at Dolores Mission School or the homeless men who sleep in the church every night—reenacts Juan Diego's encounters with the Virgin of Guadalupe at the feast day mass. Usually the priest concelebrants watch the story unfold from their seats behind the altar, which gives us the added advantage of watching the faces of the people as the narrative proceeds. When Juan Diego's uncle, Juan Bernardino, is healed of his illness, some lady in the congregation will inevitably gush to a senora next to her, "*Se alivio.*" When the roses drop from Juan Diego's tilma, people gasp like they did not see this coming.

They are not stupid people. They know this story in and out; better than most. They know how it ends. They just choose to see differently. This is a genuine instance of the Zen Buddhist concept of the "beginner's mind." The people of Dolores Mission know this iconic tale well and yet are able to stay in the story, in the moment, and this creates a vast newness. They are able to see it for the first time all over again.

"Wish me luck," says Mikey, a sixteen-year-old gang member and *chapparito*, sticking his head into my office. "I'm off to see my probation officer. I think he'll let me off probation today."

Later that afternoon, he returns and immediately slinks into one of my office chairs, clearly dejected. "*Sabes qué?* G, my probation officer is a private part."

Apparently he wanted to spare me the expletive.

"Why?" I ask. "What'd he say?"

"He told me I was a loser and I'll never amount to nuthin'."

"He said that?" I reply. "Then what did *you* say?"

"I said, 'Your mom's a basehead.'"

"Yeah, that should move him to let you off probation."

The beauty and wisdom of beginner's mind is that you don't know how it's gonna turn out. Not the Guadalupe story and not some probation officer who thinks he has a gang member pegged. Staying anchored in the here and now liberates us from having the future all figured out, for better or worse. Besides, what they say is true: "The future is not what it used to be."

Abraham is now on his third try at Homeboy. During his first two attempts, he was known as the guy who did not play well with others. His outbursts were violent and filled with rage, and would be triggered if even the slightest wrinkle appeared in his day. He didn't handle hiccups well. Based on his past performance, many folks at Homeboy thought they knew how his latest attempt would turn out. But one day, hours after our Homeboy family picnic had ended, Abraham texted me. "I enjoyed myself today," the message said. "The picnic was lovely."

I cried as I read it. Faced with the undeniable communion of our earlier gathering, Abraham chose the possibility and vastness in today's tenderness. Now: the day of salvation.

I take two cousins, Michael and Mario, both gang members recently released from detention facilities, to get new clothes. We go to the JCPenney in Huntington Park. Once we walk in, I tell them that they each have $200 to spend. I caution them to tabulate in their minds how much each item costs, so as not to go over their budget. When I tell them to go ahead and shop, they hesitate.

"Aren't ya gonna come with us?" asks Mario.

"Yeah, G," Michael adds. "We're used to being supervised." So I walk and shop with them, occasionally stopping to "supervise."

Soon enough, their arms are filled with merchandise. We head to the cashiers and get into the long line to wait to pay. Suddenly something occurs to Mario.

"I need a belt," he says. I tell him to hurry, pointing to the belt section nearby as he dumps his merchandise in my arms. A clerk opens another checkout line, and people begin to move. Standing at some distance from us, Mario drapes belts around himself, sizing up their fit. As Michael and I approach the register, Mario is still in the belt section and still indecisive. My face says to him, *Apúrate, cabrón*. "I don't know," he says loudly, with a belt loosely wrapped around him. "What do ya think?"

I'm about to tell him what I think when suddenly his cousin, in perfect King's English, says, "You look *splendid*!" I turn to Michael and my entire face seems to say, *Splendid?* Everyone in line has scrawled on their faces: *Splendid?* And the two clerks can't help themselves, "SPLENDID???" Michael demurs and looks around. "I don't know, I heard it on TV once."

The prophet Baruch tells us, "God will show all the earth your splendor." But will it be attentive long enough to notice? "Rise up in splendor."

Once, Homeboy was given a handful of tickets to a movie screening at Walt Disney Studios in Burbank. I took three homies with me, young guys in need of being snatched up, otherwise they'd be prowling in the projects. One of them, Artie, was something of a know-it-all, always with an answer at the ready. On the drive over, one of the group was curious about the ethnic background of a homie at the office. "What race is he?" the kid asked.

"Catholic," Artie replied.

The subject then turned to "the strangest thing you've ever eaten." Everyone made a contribution: rattlesnake and alligator were mine.

Artie, with a quickness, said, "You know, they're both aphrodisiacs."

"Really?" I asked, wanting to push the limits here. "Why don't you explain to everyone what an aphrodisiac is."

And, as I have done in every oral exam I've ever taken, Artie, extemporizing confidently, explained: "Well, it's a disiac . . . with a mean-ass fro." The guys in the backseat nodded their heads. You learn something new every day.

We arrived at the studio. As we drove through, we noticed statues of the seven dwarfs appearing to hold up the roof on the facade of one of the buildings. A guard came out to direct us to the theater.

"You're on Mickey now," he said. "Go two blocks and turn left on Goofy." I feel like, for most of my life, I've been "taking a left on Goofy." The homies took it all in as we made our way to the screening.

"Hey, whatever happened to that fool Walt Disney, anyway?" one of them asked.

"Oh, he's dead," Artie said. "But I heard they froze his ass— you know, until they find a cure for dead people."

We are called to a vigilance in the here and now. We try to sniff out significance and marvel at all those things we daily take for granted. Until they find the cure for dead people, it's the best we can do.

————

Marquis is in his early twenties, an unsmiling, imposing gang member who spent chunks of childhood and all of his adolescence behind bars. The last five years, before he settled in at Homeboy Industries, were spent with the Youth Authority, a correctional system in California that puts the shellac on "hardened." Marquis certainly

brought that hardness with him when he began with us, embody-
ing the sentiment I once read in a faux letter of recommendation:
"Works well when under constant supervision and cornered like a
rat in a trap." It got better for him, though. Like most who enter
our portals, Marquis found tenderness at every turn, and it rein-
troduced him to his estranged childhood. Every now and then,
buoyancy would make guest appearances in this exceedingly tough
gangster.

Once I was poring over something at my desk when I looked
up and saw him in his white Homeboy Bakery uniform, the shirt
smudged with great smears of chocolate icing. Before I could say
anything, he tossed his hands up in the air, in an overly fey display,
and exclaimed, "Voilà!" Now, if there is a more incongruous thing
a gang member can say upon entering a room than "Voilà!" I have
not heard it. To this day it is how Marquis and I always greet each
other. His very being and utterance of this word seem to enliven
what Walt Whitman wrote: "I am larger, better than I thought, / I
did not know I held such goodness."

Voilà.

Scripture reminds us, constantly, that we are meant not to wait for
salvation but to watch for it today. Heaven, then, is not a promise we
await but a practice we fully engage in. What is entirely available to
us is the Kingdom of God, or what the Buddhists call "Pure Land."

Outside a cemetery chapel, while we silently await a coffin to
be placed in a hearse, I see a young girl of three or four across from
me who's *inquieta*. In an attempt to reduce her fidgeting, her mom
reaches into a large bag, takes out a beautiful, ripe pear, and hands
it to her daughter. The girl twirls the pear around, observing every
part of it—first right-side up, then upside down. She considers this
pear in the morning sunshine, then asks her dad quietly, "How do
you open it?"

It's a good question. How do we open our hearts and minds to a new way of thinking? How do we open a path toward a transformed life? How can our eyes be opened? One need not have been there to imagine how the father answered his daughter's question: "Take a big ol' bite."

Yeah . . . look before you leap . . . but leap. Richard Rohr was right: "We don't think ourselves into a new way of living. We live ourselves into a new way of thinking." How do I open it—to live fully in recovery without self-medicating; to find my own light by walking through my own darkness; to love my kids more than I hate my enemies? Take a big ol' bite, even if you don't know exactly how to open it. Leap, and the net will appear.

We find ourselves on the lookout for moments of spaciousness and calm, when our hearts can be restored again to a place of beauty, innocence, and wholeness. Then we can hear what the Sufis call "the voice of the Beloved."

Our employment services folks are able to place Alvaro, after his eighteen months with us, as a general-labor shipper at a fabric company. Several weeks into the job, he notices the database the company uses for shipping is one he's familiar with from a previous experience. He lets his boss know. When he's asked where he learned it, he takes a deep breath and responds, tentatively, "When I was locked up?" His boss asks to see. So Alvaro shows him. He navigates the database with ease, and two days later the boss hands him an envelope, which he thinks for sure are his marching papers. Instead, it is notice of a $5.75 hourly raise, effective immediately.

In Mark's gospel, Jesus cures a deaf man. He says, "Be opened," and things that have previously held the man back, an inability to hear and speak, are lifted. We identify those things that close our hearts—grasping and anger, fear and pride—and turn to our world, instead, with a tender heart. We're opened. We find the ability to be with anguish and pain without having to control or change it.

Having just finished mass at the Youth Authority facility in Whittier, I'm walking to my car in the parking lot. Out of the early evening darkness, I hear a homie yell from his grated window, "Drive safe, G!" I am certain that this unknown kid rediscovered, in this extension of self, the power of the tender heart. "Happiness," Thich Nhat Hanh tells us, "only comes from kindness and compassion." I have no doubt this kid withdrew from the bars of that window and rested in that happiness.

Homeboy receives people; it doesn't rescue them. In being received rather than rescued, gang members come to find themselves at home in their own skin. Homeboy's message is not "You can measure up someday." Rather, it is: "Who you are is enough." And when you have enough, you have plenty. In this effort, we are always paying attention and are obedient to that. The word "obey" has its origin in "listening." It is difficult to truly and deeply listen. When a homie is sitting in front of my desk, the mantra on a continuous loop in my head is "Stay listening." Another handy one is "Now. Here. This." Listen here and now and only to this person.

Before entering our eighteen-month program, and even after they are accepted, homies are drug tested. Embarking on "the good journey" requires confronting the inevitable emotional obstacles in that path. It's always a painful process, and we don't want them to numb themselves by self-medication. Once they let go of the hatred for their gang rivals—every homie's starting point—they are left to deal with their own pain.

"I'm at a pitchfork in my life," a program candidate tells me. (Good thing I speak homie, so I know what he means.) "I've decided to be determined."

I ask him if he'll test clean.

"All I have in my system is hope," he says. "I will test positive for that."

The hope found here is like the genesis of a pathway in the countryside. At first there is nothing there but tall grass, but as hundreds upon hundreds walk through that grass, a direction emerges that others can follow. If love is the answer, community is the context, and tenderness the methodology. Otherwise, love stays in the head or, worse, hovers above it. Or it stays in the heart, which is never enough. For unless love becomes tenderness—the connective tissue of love—it never becomes transformational. The tender doesn't happen tomorrow . . . only now.

Just the other day, a trainee said to me, "Never ever in my life have I felt surrounded by love—till now . . . till here." There is nothing more essential, vital, and important than love and its carrier—tenderness—practiced in the present moment. By keeping it close, just right now, we are reminded to choose connection over alienation, kinship over self-absorption.

We need only meet the world, today, with a loving heart, to determine what we will find. A loving heart doesn't color your world like rose-colored glasses; it alters it. William James wrote, "The greatest revolution of our generation is the discovery that human beings, by changing the inner attitudes of their minds, can change the outer aspects of their lives."

Daja, my "runner" for the day, walks in to tell me who is next to see me. He sports a wild Afro and is a gentle soul (unlike the guy who just left my office, who was not quite so gentle—a homie thick with belligerence and a jagged edge).

"Gosh, Daja, why can't people be more like you?" I ask as he turns to show the next visitor in.

He chuckles. "And here I'm tryin' to be more like 'people.'"

———

No matter who it is—Mike Wallace, Tom Brokaw, Dr. Phil—there always comes a moment during the interview when they turn on the hard-hitting, journalistic counterpunch to show the viewers that their segment isn't just about full-blown admiration. Usually they toss in a criticism gleaned from conversations with contrarians—in my case, usually cops. I'm sitting in my office with Anderson Cooper when he says, "The police say you're naïve. That gang members take advantage of you."

I always have the same answer at the ready: "How can someone take my advantage when I'm giving it?" (Years later, in another interview with Cooper, this time sitting in our brand-new bakery, he tells me he remembers my answer and uses it himself from time to time with his friends. I thank him and ask if I'm due any royalties.) We so fear being duped, yet much of that comes from being a stranger to our own wounds.

Once, in a Homeboy Council meeting, the daily homie senior staff meeting to discuss the trainees, a kid is mentioned who has been behaving badly. The staff is weighing in on what they've observed of the kid. One homie staff is sure of himself.

"You know what his problem is?" he says. "He thinks his shit don't stink."

But another homie offers, "No . . . all he smells IS stink." If we don't welcome our own wounds, then overconfidence in our own savviness, and fear of being taken advantage of, tempts us to despise the wounded.

But if one's wounds are near at hand, it leads to compassionate understanding and makes kindness more readily available right now. "Love is the eye," Hugh of Saint Victor writes. It is our lens and way of seeing. It is the answer and solution to our shortsightedness, on those days when we can't see straight. I have never seen anything so able to defuse a burst of violence or the spewing of hate or the indifference to those in pain than love shown in a kind word, gesture, stance, and presence. It is a way of being possible only in the present moment. Like the gentle rocking of a colicky baby, loving-kindness, as the homies say, "kicks in."

Largo has gotten a job as "social coordinator" at an old folks' home. He's in my office at night with other homies and I ask him how it is.

"I hate it," he tells us. "Damn, G, I mean, old people, they be bugging. They always be walkin' slow." He gets up and demonstrates. "You're behind 'em and sayin' to yourself: 'Let's goooo. Let's goooo.' And their teeth always be fallin' out. Disgusting. And they always be cheating at bingo." The homies are really laughing now. "And they always be yellin', 'Bingo! Bingo!' and I have to walk up to 'em and say, 'No, you do not have Bingo.' In fact, that's what it be soundin' like when their teeth be fallin' out: *bing-O*." It's a winning performance, and everyone is slain with laughter.

Later, though, when it's just the two of us, Largo's tenderness makes a timely arrival.

"Actually, G, I love them old people. Don't know where I'd be without 'em. I look forward to showin' up every day." Kindness ventilating our self-absorption, moments of rage, and the distance we create between ourselves and the broken. Works every time.

I once presided at the funeral of two brothers, Miguel and Cesar, both gunned down not far from their home. Two caskets were lined up together in the church, symbols of a heartbreak beyond my ability to describe. The pain was palpable, like walking into a furnace room at peak capacity: you can only stay inside briefly before the heat forces you to rush outside, sweaty and gasping for air.

Before and during the service, it rained. And not just a drizzle— gale-force, hurricane winds with water flying everywhere at end-of-the-world magnitude. After communion, the boys' father rose to speak and gestured to the ceiling, the noise of rain pummeling the roof making him barely audible.

"*Los cielos están llorando,*" he managed to say. The heavens are crying. Then he pointed to the two coffins, side by side, like the beds in the room they shared. There was a pause. "Don't lose one day," he continued. "Don't let a day go by that you don't pay attention to your kids. Don't waste time in '*Aquí mando yo*'—['I call shots around here']. Our children are loaned to us. They belong to God, and they will return to God. Don't waste one day in not loving them."

From the church, it was a twenty-mile procession to the cemetery. The rain continued, the kind that defies windshield wipers at even their highest speeds. That is, until we pulled into the cemetery, where the rain just stopped. After five hours of constant pounding, nothing. And more than that, the sun didn't just peek out—it pushed all clouds aside and warmed the earth. The sun reminded us, as we laughed and held each other in this graveyard, that the only antidote to our misery is to stay in the present. This present is eternal, and the only eternity that counts is now. "This is the first, wildest, and wisest thing I know: that the soul exists, and that it is built entirely out of attentiveness," Mary Oliver writes. A grieving father and a warm, surprising sun reminded us that, indeed, paying attention, right now, leads us all to soulful living.

I take two homegirls, Shameeka and Abby, on a speaking trip to San Francisco. They are big girls, tattooed gang members who have been in prison. You would not want to mess with these two— they know how to handle themselves. At the airport, I'm finishing up with the woman at Enterprise Car Rental. Shameeka and Abby, wearing very large sweatshirts emblazoned with the Homeboy logo, are standing off at a distance. I'm wearing a button-down shirt embroidered with the same logo.

"May I ask you a question?" the Enterprise employee asks. I nod. "What's Homeboy Industries?"

I explain that it's the largest gang intervention, rehab, and reentry program in the world. "And these two ladies," I say, pointing to Shameeka and Abby, "are gonna help me give a talk to a thousand judges in San Francisco."

"Awesome." She then adds perkily, "Would you like me to put them down as additional drivers?"

"Are you out of your mind?" I deadpan, but everyone in earshot, including the homegirls, laugh.

As we head to our rental car, the girls trail behind and I can hear Shameeka quietly squeak to the rental car lady: "Thanks for tryin'."

Before my lunchtime keynote to the judges the next day, we give a workshop to a group of them. I simply introduce Shameeka and Abby, who take center stage. They are present in their stories, pausing often to cry as they share the terror of their lives: torture, abuse, abandonment, and violence. They both speak of their addictions and that particular pain of having given birth in the midst of them, then having their kids snatched and raised by strangers. The judges are riveted, and at the end they stand and applaud. Truly, awe came upon everyone.

We fly home that afternoon. Back in my car in the Burbank Airport parking lot, I call my then eighty-seven-year-old mother to tell her that I'm home, a travel ritual of ours.

"Tell me again what you were doin' in San Francisco?" she asks.

"We were giving a talk to a bunch a judges," I answer, "and these two wonderful women helped me give a workshop." After some more chatting, we say good-bye and I hang up. After a moment Shameeka, sitting in the front seat, lets out a "Huh."

"What?" I ask.

"Oh, nothing."

"No. What?"

"Well, just right now, you called us 'wonderful women.'"

"Yeah? So?"

Shameeka enters some quiet, soulful place. "I don't know," she begins slowly. "When you say it," she turns to look me in the eyes. "I believe you."

See something. Say something. They'll believe you. The time for any of us to be returned to ourselves is now. The ground beneath our feet is the Kingdom of God, the Pure Land. It's not around the corner, it *is* the corner. Kinship is not a reward bestowed at the end. It's here, it's now, it's at hand and within our reach. And this moment is the only one available to us.

In Advent time, we are reminded over and over again: "Stay awake." This is not a warning that death is coming but a reminder that life is happening. Now . . . is the day of salvation. We see as God sees: with amplitude, wideness, and mercy. The only moment left to us to participate in this larger love, this limitless, all-accepting love, is in the present moment.

Can you hear it? The voice of the Beloved.

CHAPTER FIVE

Sell Your Cleverness

Every day, we encourage the homies and homegirls to tell their stories. They visit elementary schools, conferences, college criminology classes—wherever—refining and improving their stories with each experience. They are tales of wisdom, of what they used to be like, of what happened to them, and what they're like now. Rumi addresses God in this poem: "The minute I heard my first love story, I started looking for you . . ." I think the same may well be true the moment you tell your first story.

Some homies get quite good at speaking. One night I had dinner with a homie named Mike. He has become so proficient at public speaking for Homeboy Industries that he has started giving me tips. "You have to pepper your talk," he tells me, "with self-defecating humor."

"Yeah," I say, "no shit."

This is a chapter on humility. Not the kind that requires "self-defecating," a beating up of oneself until one's esteem is leveled beyond recognition. Rather, it is the humility that can lead to a peaceful surrender and a pervasive sense of gratitude. It is the natural terrain of connection with another, and how we are to arrive at a place of cherishing in kinship. It is, as they say in business, not a "downsizing" but a "right-sizing."

Joshua wants to coin a catchphrase like those made famous on television—something like "Dy-no-MITE" or "We are two wild and crazy guys" or "What'chu talkin' 'bout, Willis?" He wants to be known for a line, and say it often enough that folks will incorporate it into their daily argot. Joshua is a tall, foot-above-everybody-else homie, and a most *guero*-looking former gang member, chiseled and striking, one of those people who can accelerate to affection faster than anybody I know. His catchphrase, which he says whenever he hugs you—and after he's planted a wet one on your cheek—is "I love your life." He's not wanting to trade his life for yours. He's simply trying to quicken you to some greater grateful embracing of what you have. It's sweet.

Another phrase Joshua uses quite a bit is his answer when asked, "Why didn't THAT take you to THAT place?" For instance, one day he returned to the Homeboy office after a meeting with his parole officer. The PO had humiliated him in front of three other officers in such a degrading and jaw-dropping way, one would not have blamed him if he had gone to "that place." But he just took it. I asked how he could, and he said, simply, "If you're humble, you'll never stumble." Another catchphrase is born. To this day I use it as a mantra to calm myself down.

If seen right, humility brings us to our true home. It grounds us in putting first things recognizably first. It anchors us in the truth of who we are. We can acknowledge that it is good to be "put in our place." "The true way to be humble is not to stoop until you're smaller than yourself," Phillips Brooks writes, "but to stand at your real height against some higher nature . . ." Right-sizing is always easier said than done.

The annual Homeboy Family Picnic is a glorious affair. I always say that heaven won't be much different than this event, when we take over an entire park with anywhere between eight hundred and one thousand staff, trainees, spouses, and kids. The picnic's first year, I'd been going through chemo and my body was coursing with steroids, which heightens your energy and emotions. You feel possessed of superhero powers. I was forever on the lookout for a grandmother pinned under a Buick so I could fling it off her.

I'd watch the softball games, teams made up of former enemies who were now working together. During one in particular, I saw the shortstop pat the second baseman on the back. My steroid-infused self would get misty-eyed, thinking of how, years ago, this *vato* had stabbed the man he was now embracing. I knew all the backstories of these players. It was all overwhelming enough to send me, occasionally, to hide behind a tree and sob.

As magical as the day can be, though, there's always one guy who threatens to disrupt things. We announce the "There will be no drinking at the picnic" rule days before the event, but there's always one homie who will bring a backpack snug with forty-ouncers and one of those red plastic cups he fills all day long.

As the picnic winds down, word makes its way to me that Chepo is very *pedo* (drunk) and is starting fights. No less than four times, he stops and yells at one of the senior staff, homies who now run the place. "You think this is funny?" he mutters as I try to escort him out of the park. People stop and stare as he staggers away from me. Of course, no one is finding this funny, but nonetheless he still finds a reason to stumble up to a guy and—*wham*—"right in the kisser," as Jackie Gleason used to say. Each time, I watch the homie on the receiving end of the *golpe* just stand there, iron-jawed and unflinching, as he takes the punch. A little bit stunned and wobbly, sure, but nonetheless, refusing to respond in kind. The stiffness of their jaws seemed to announce, *You cannot take me to that place.* Chepo's rage and concomitant punches have no power over them. Each one takes the hit and then, truly, turns the other cheek. It's remarkable to behold.

The picnic always happens on payday, so I escort the fist wielder to the park's entrance so he will leave quietly. It's just the two of us, and I have his paycheck.

"Dog, look," I begin. "Just take your check, go home, sleep it off, and we'll talk tomorrow." Chepo finds his footing as best he can and points at the check, refusing to accept it.

"You can take that check and shove it up your ass," he mumbles with a great flourish of shoving gestures.

"In that case," I reply, "if you change your mind, you know where you can find it."

Okay. He took me to that place.

Mystics ask God to remind them that they are nothing. This is irritating to the ego's need for self-importance. Holy men and women knew that it was precisely the "smallness" that gave way to favored entrance into kinship. Juan Diego, to whom Our Lady of Guadalupe appeared, described himself this way: "I am a nobody. I am a short rope. A small ladder. The tail end. A leaf." Modern eyes roll at such a display of humility, but there is something exhilarating in finding our right size in our thorough insignificance.

There is no end to folks who help me find my true height in my nothingness.

The kids are filing out of the chapel at Sylmar Juvenile Hall and I shake their hands as they return to their units. One of the girls stops and asks me, "Have you ever heard of Homeboy Industries?" Now, keep in mind, I may have mentioned Homeboy Industries once or twice (or eight times) during my homily.

"Yeah," I answer, "I think I may have heard of it."

She redoubles her enthusiasm. "Have you ever read *Tattoos on the Heart*? It's amazing."

I tell her that not only did I read it—I wrote it.

She releases her hand from mine and stares at me for a couple beats. "You did not." Her face is now a grimace. I hand her my card and ask her to check the name on the card with the name on the book. She interrogates the card, looks up, not at all pleased. "You did not," she repeats before walking away.

It is liberating to be brought back to one's insignificance. We are allowed to abandon the pretense that we are more than we are and find comfort in knowing that we are enough. We hand over our self-dramatizing intensity and the need to get the seat of honor and find the thrill that is in our "place"—in the last row and worst seat. "Sell your cleverness," Rumi writes, "and buy bewilderment." Like Jesus, who emptied himself, this humility keeps us from clinging to power and our own cleverness. In our raw need, we find our true selves and discover the misery there is in ceaselessly needing validation.

We still need to contend with the original prejudice that some people are important and others don't count. Our ego clings to self-importance and puts us on a path that draws us further from our soul's truth. Humility can keep us from moving into this territory.

Back in the mid-1990s, Vice President Al Gore visited Homeboy. He was scheduled to tour the childcare center, then walk across the street to see the original Homeboy Bakery and have a roundtable discussion with the homies. Security, as you can imagine, was quite extensive, and to manage it the parish offices were taken over by the Secret Service a couple of days before the party arrived. Since President Clinton was in Europe that week, the "football" with launch codes for nuclear weapons traveled with Gore. The briefcase—and the military aide who carried it—needed its own office. So I gave him mine.

Accompanied by the group was a bomb-sniffing dog who, frankly, thought he was "all that." He strutted along and seemed to have one of those lapel devices with the curly cord leading to his ear. (I thought the shades were a bit much.) He proceeded into our garage with more hubris than I think a dog ought to have. The garage was where our homeless men, who sleep in the church, watched TV and played cards. There was a "barrio" cat that had been adopted by the homeless men, and no sooner had this Secret Service dog entered than he found himself fleeing the scene, whimpering and whining, with the ghetto feline in full pursuit. The crowds behind the rope line loved the comeuppance.

On the morning of the visit, we greeted the vice president as his limousine pulled up in front of the day care center. The crowd waved and screamed as he stepped out of the limo. He had just come from the airport, and after the greetings and niceties he eyeballed a room that looks like it might be a restroom. Excusing himself, before anyone could tell him otherwise, he darted into it.

Now, those of us who knew the lay of the land did the "slo-mo no": NOOOOOOOO!! The vice president had stepped into a bathroom all right, but one reserved for the tiniest of kids, with several minuscule toilets, not even a foot off the ground. If he had to go "number two," we might have had an international incident on our hands.

The homies chosen to have a conversation with the vice president were, of course, carefully vetted by the Secret Service beforehand. One of my bakers, Freddy, was denied participation by the advance team due to a tussle he had once had with a police officer. The report they cited said he had kicked the officer in the shins during an arrest, and though no assault charges were filed, it seemed enough reason to exclude him. I asked the gentleman in charge of the security detail if he thought Freddy would pose any danger to the life of the vice president.

"No, we got that covered," he said, and chuckled, explaining how, before he entered, metal detectors and sharpshooters would be in place on the premises.

"Well, then," I said, having anticipated this response, "if you don't think this young man threatens the life of the vice president, then isn't your job done?"

The agent moved closer and seemed to know how he would answer this even before he was asked it. He didn't want Freddy present, he said, "because, Father, I don't want anyone to take a picture of this scumbag and the vice president of the United States. Simple."

I called the White House to complain. They investigated, and when they called me back, they told me there was nothing they could do. I had to tell Freddy that he was disinvited. He was characteristically sweet and seemed more upset that I was, rather than because he was being excluded. "Oh, G, don't sweat it," he said. "I kinda didn't think I'd be allowed to go anyway."

If you're humble, you'll never stumble.

Surely a measure of our kinship will always rest in the certainty that no life holds more value than another. I was once part of a protest trying to stop the execution of the next inmate on San Quentin's death row, a man who had killed a police officer. At a counter-demonstration the following day, LA County sheriff Lee Baca addressed the previous day's protest.

"Do they mean to tell us," he asked, "that the life of the man who killed a cop is worth more than the life he took?" Well, no. Not more, but the same. To think otherwise is to mire ourselves in the opposite of kinship, in a world where not everyone belongs.

With only three days' notice, Homeboy was informed that President Obama wanted to visit with some homies during his upcoming visit to Los Angeles. Coming to our headquarters was deemed too "porous" and difficult to secure. (I guess Joe Biden never got the memo.) We were told to submit the names of four trainees who would be allowed to attend a meet and greet with the president after his speech at Los Angeles Trade-Tech.

On the hottest August day in memory, the homies and I walked past the crowd of people waiting for the speech. When we got to the front of the line, which snaked around the block, we saw a local elected official trying to get in as a VIP. He was pleading with the Secret Service agents. I knew him and vouched for him to try and help the situation, to no avail. But when I told the same agent that we were from Homeboy, we were immediately waved in. These four gang members, needless to say, were beside themselves.

"You know," one said, "not just anybody gets to meet the president. Not even rap stars. Not even Lil' J." (I had to google him.)

"How much ya wanna bet," another replied, "he'll say, 'Don't call me Mr. President, call me Barack'?" (he didn't). We were given yellow wristbands and escorted to the shaded VIP section, where we had seats to view the president's speech; the rest of the crowd, including the aggrieved official, was left to stand in a shadeless, sweltering patch of brown grass in front of the stage.

A striking black woman began to sing the National Anthem and Johnny, the homie standing next to me, leaned in and whispered, "I don't know how to explain what's happening to me right now." I encouraged him to give it a try. "I mean, just right now I don't know, I got chills." The sensation, I knew, was not caused by a sudden burst of patriotism but a palpable wave of gracious inclusion. This is the sound of someone previously outside being given the welcome mat to enter inside.

After the speech, White House staff ushered us and the young people from other at-risk youth organizations into a tiny, airless room adorned with flags and a plain backdrop screen. Moments later the president entered and began meeting everyone, asking for their names and ages as he did so. The White House photographer captured the moment as Obama shook hands and shared a word with each one. He got to our very own Herbert, a tall, lanky nineteen-year-old African American who worked in our diner at City Hall. Herbert had a beard that looked like Brillo pads caught in a windstorm. The day before we had tried to give him a razor, but he refused it. The president greeted him after the introduction.

"Herbert," he said, smiling, "I wish that at nineteen, I could have grown a beard like that. Heck, I wish I could grow one right now." (Vindicated, Herbert sent an "I told you so" sneer in my general direction.) He asked what Herbert did at Homeboy.

"I work at the diner," Herbert said. "But I mainly work on myself," he quickly added. "You know, therapy, anger management, stuff like that."

The leader of the free world paused. Then he shook Herbert's hand again and said, "I commend you."

I was the last one to shake the president's hand. "Father Greg Boyle," I told him. "I'm sixty years old." Everyone laughed. The president pointed a finger at me.

"And you don't look a day over fifty-nine," he said, to more laughter. Before the visit ended, he shared a bit about his own life. "My mother was a single mom," he said. "I got in trouble, just never got caught." It was a tender and vulnerable moment. Later I heard a homie say, "He was one of us."

That day four gang members shook the hand of the president of the United States. The commander-in-chief. The most powerful man on earth. And even *he* is not more important than the homies whose hands he shook in that airless room.

———————

Our fragile ego gets nicked and yet we are called again to the joy of self-forgetting. "Unless you become like these children," Jesus says, it's hard to enter into the kinship to which we are all invited. The best you can hope for, sometimes, is to completely enjoy the trip home to the humble place.

Years ago, before the "Internets," when you wanted to travel, you called a travel agent. Mine was Robert, a wonderfully kind and solicitous fellow who always called me "Father."

"Call me Greg," I'd tell him.

"Yes, Father," he'd reply.

I was flying enough and had seemed to sell my soul to American Airlines, so Robert said he would apply for an AAdvantage card for me. Apparently, on the application he put my name as "Father Gregory Boyle"—spelling out the whole of "Father," along with the entirety of my name. Of course, there wasn't room for all, so American Airlines abbreviated it as anyone would, so that it would fit. The card arrived in the mail, and read "Fat Gregory Boyle." Every time I would hand the card to the folks at the airport counter, they'd look at the card, then at me, quite sympathetically, perhaps thinking that the company had somehow "scarlet-lettered" me for being overly fond of double-bacon cheeseburgers. I always enjoyed the touchstone nature of it: handing the card to someone and being returned to myself by way of the humble path. Some would call it "not taking yourself too seriously." The Buddhists would say it keeps you "playful and free."

There's a story about the opening night of *A Streetcar Named Desire* on Broadway. The critics were going crazy, and a reporter went to the stage door to get a comment from someone in the cast. They found an actor and asked what the play was about. The actor told him, "It's a play about a man who comes to take a woman away to a mental institution." We are like this sometimes. That was that actor's part, and in his self-absorption it was all he needed to know. In our narcissistic, ego-clinging mind-set, we can't see the whole play because we're too absorbed in our role in it. The homies have always jostled me out of my self-absorption. They are masters at it.

A homie texts me to ask where I am.

"Kansas," I text back. "You know, tornadoes."

"Yeah," he writes back. "Tornadoes. They're caused by hot air. You'll fit right in there."

Another time, I'm driving to East Max, a facility of the county jail system in Los Angeles, for a mass that begins at the unthinkable hour of 8:00 p.m. on a Friday. The 5 Freeway on a Friday night in Los Angeles might as well be a used-car lot, because no one is moving anywhere anytime soon.

About a hundred inmates are gathering and settling for mass when I arrive, late. We are in a large dining hall that smells of an odd mixture of "Pina-Sol" and refried beans beyond their expiration date. A vaguely menacing character approaches me before I can make it to the front of the room. He's over six feet, muscled, and inked up all over.

"So," he glowers and nods, "you're the famous Father Greg. G-Dog." This last name is surrounded by aggressive air quotes. "I know aaaaallllllll about you," he says, his head bouncing up and down like he now has all the evidence he needs to convict me before a jury of my peers. "Your reputation exceeds you."

I let him down gently, suggesting he is not the first person who thinks this, including myself.

A homegirl, Lisa, comes to visit me and she brings her son, who is in the first grade at Dolores Mission School. She stands in front of my desk and we catch up on each other's lives. I knew her back in the day, before motherhood, when she was a wild woman fully dedicated to her gang. All during our conversation, her son is staring at me, mouth agape, appearing to be in something of a trance. He tugs on his mom's T-shirt and says, "Mom, for Halloween, I'm gonna dress like Father Greg." This cracks us both up.

"Why?" Lisa asks.

"Cuz the teacher says that we have to come to school dressed like a saint." This slays us.

Lisa bends down to eye level with her son. "Hon-ey," she steadily explains, "Father Greg is no saint."

Thank you. Thank you very much.

The root meanings of the word "embarrassment" are "blockage," "obstacle," and "impediment" to thought or action. We can feel blocked from the eventual liberation of "humbling ourselves" by clinging to the sting of embarrassment and by lamenting our red-faced horror of being singled out. We can feel impeded from the transformation that comes from having a different lens from which to view things.

Growing up, I attended St. Brendan's, a parochial school run by the BVM nuns. I think I knew back then that BVM stood for "Blessed Virgin Mary" but we students preferred to use "Black Veiled Monsters." My fifth-grade teacher was—let's call her "Sister Mary Mary," as my dad called all the nuns. Sister Mary Mary was tall and lanky and, like all the sisters, dressed from head to toe in a black habit. We sat alphabetically, and "Boyle" was in the row closest to the side blackboard. One day Sister Mary Mary came to my side of the room to write a lengthy assignment on the board, doing so rapidly and with high energy. As she wrote, her rear end seemed to be motorized, and the tiny pleats of her full-length habit gyrated as she moved back and forth. It looked like, under all the black fabric, she had one of those paint-can-shaking machines you see at the hardware store—two cans shaking.

I was something of a class clown back then, so, to get the attention of my fellow students, I took my pencil and gestured at Sister Mary Mary as if I were poking her fast-moving butt. The class roared with laughter and she quickly turned around. My fellow students, of course, wouldn't give me up. She returned to her writing. Next I took my ruler and pretended to thwack her derriere. The class couldn't help themselves. Again she turned and again we silenced the laughter. I was enjoying this attention greatly. So finally I took my eyes off the target to look toward my classmates, held up the back of my hand, mugging like a vaudevillian, and, suddenly, connected so powerfully with her body that everyone was more stunned than amused. The nun turned slowly to me.

"Mr. Boyle," she said, "may I help you?"

You learn with the years to abide in the sting, then move quickly away to the equanimity of humility. You don't want to stay stuck in embarrassment. And yet whatever leads us to recognize our "nothingness" hastens our falling into the arms of God. This, in turn, issues in a cherishing of the other that is not possible otherwise.

In a packed church in Escondido, California, I was sitting in the front pew as the event's organizer, a very energetic woman, was introducing me. She clearly wanted to galvanize the assembled troops into action, imploring them to take whatever message I was about to deliver and use it to improve their community. As she spoke, she consulted the notes she'd written on large index cards. Once she got midway through her speech, however, she started to speak more from the heart, ignoring the cards in front of her.

"So, finally," she said, "before we get Father Greg up here, I invite you to get involved and live your faith. For as Father Greg says so eloquently in his book *Tattoos on the Heart,* 'God does not love you.'" The entire room sucked in air. Had I been on a TV sitcom, I would have done a "spit take," spraying the woman with a beverage. She hurriedly conferred with her index cards. "No, that can't be right," she muttered, looking for the card she had jettisoned when she went extemporaneous on us. "Oh, here it is. 'Not only does God love us, it is His joy to love us.' Well, that's entirely different." Laughter shook the room.

While I suppose the woman reddened some at her error, she mainly took her place humbly. The crowd enveloped her, cherished her as God does, and quickly transformed the speed bump of this embarrassment into a rich laughter that transported and elevated us all. The packed church instinctively sought to remind her of our essential belonging and her unshakable status within it.

The whole world can love you, hoist you on its shoulders, wave palm fronds wildly as you enter town, and "like" you countless times on Facebook. But one person raises an eyebrow in our general direction, and we unravel. Just one person, unbelievably, has that power. While we long to be lost in God's love, we often get lost in the one person who doesn't like us, or in the homie who is disappointed in me, or in clinging to one's reputation and what people think.

Apparently, Larry David, the actor from *Curb Your Enthusiasm*, was taken by friends to Yankee Stadium on his birthday. His buddies informed the stadium officials of this special occasion, and, near the seventh-inning stretch, his mug, live from the stadium, was projected on the Jumbotron. The entire place gave him a standing ovation and a "Happy Birthday" serenade, with great hooting and hollering. But later, in the parking lot, a guy drove by and shouted out, "Hey, Larry! You suck." This completely undid David, who spent the rest of the evening obsessing about this guy. "Why would that guy say that?" he kept asking. "What was that about?" One guy.

We all clamor for praise and recoil at blame. They are oddly and equally seductive. They pull us away from our center, and yet we strangely have grown dependent on blame and praise. Instead, we have to find our way to notice and return. Notice the positive sheen of praise and still refuse to cling to it. Choose to move quickly back to the center. Let the pang of this blame wash over you, abide in it, and then return immediately to your center. We want the "bliss of blamelessness," as the Buddha would say, and yet find ourselves attaching to the praise of the crowd or the surly comment of the disgruntled. We try and gently catch ourselves when we're about to let resentment harden into blame and let the illusion of praise define who we are.

I have long found myself the receptacle of a great deal of transference. I try not to take it personally. Certainly, to a host of homies,

I am this "father figure"—lately, homies have taken to calling me "Pops." There are times when I make my way through a room after a talk and people can be over-the-top effusive in their praise. The requests for selfies sometimes exceed some legal limit. You have to decide not to take adulation personally. People will project all this on to you, and surely it's not about you.

As that is true, so is the opposite. One time I received some big award at the Biltmore Hotel in Los Angeles. When the dinner event ended, I was instantly swamped by people, being asked to shake hands, sign copies of my book, and pose for pictures. At one point, as I slowly inched my way toward the exit, I turned to my right and saw an elegantly dressed middle-aged woman who got so close to me I could smell the wine on her breath. She smiled and pulled herself in tightly.

"I hate you," she said, steel in each word. "I hate everything you stand for. I despise what Homeboy Industries represents. My son was killed by a gang member. I have nothing but hate for you and your organization, and I always will."

I was stunned, speechless. I managed to touch her arm and say "I'm sorry" before she walked away. I felt less that I had been in the presence of a grieving mother and more that I had had an encounter with an imprisoned one. How I would have longed to allow her to tell me the whole story, unfiltered, and perhaps become a passageway for her. Nonetheless, it returned me to my true home, anchored and grounded far from any adulation. It was a shocking and sad moment, and though the sting was sharp, I knew not to take it personally. The more you take things personally, the more you suffer. You observe it, hold it up to the light, release it, and move on. One can choose to let suffering be the elevator to a heightened place of humble loving. You adjust the knot on the red string around your wrist and find your center again.

Humility returns the center of gravity to the center. It addresses the ego clinging, which supplies oxygen to our suffering. It calls for a light grasp. For the opposite of clinging is not letting go but cherishing. This is the goal of the practice of humility. That having a "light grasp" on life prepares the way for cherishing what is right in front of us.

One of my great friends, Jeanette Van Vleck, CSJ, taught me the notion of the "light grasp." We met each other in the late 1970s and together we attended protests of the nuclear arms race and the war in El Salvador. We even got arrested together. She was the champion of the idea of not holding on to things, and yet, by her own admission, struggled with it all her life. Clinging was the constant of the suffering she endured. It gave her, as Jack Kornfield calls it, "rope burn." Indeed, at its worst, clinging kept her from cherishing.

One time we went to the Grove in LA, saw a movie, and then ate at a fancy Chinese restaurant next door to the theater. Three days later she called me. "You're not gonna believe this," she said. "After we had dinner, the next day, I wasn't feeling well. I went to the doctor. Now, you're not gonna believe this. The doctor says I have acute leukemia." I was silent. Then she added, "I'm never going to *that* Chinese restaurant again."

We howled for a very long time.

When I told that story at her funeral just thirty days later, I told the packed church that Jeanette had arrived, finally, at the "light grasp." Turns out, when you are bound by nothing, you can go beyond sorrow. It can't get a foothold. As the ad for Napster once put it: "Own nothing, have everything." Humility can prepare the soil that leads you to rely on nothing until you want nothing. No clinging and a light grasp. Entering into the kinship of God requires humility.

Andres was abandoned by his mother when he was nine years old and left homeless for a couple of years. He has always been a clear example for me of the soul's deepest longing to inhabit its truth. The one thing he wanted, more than anything, was to improve his vocabulary. "I was enumerating all the things I needed to do today," he'd say. Then he'd add, "Enumerating means to make a list." If he agrees with me, he says, "I concur." He actually told a roomful of shrinks during a talk in San Diego that at Homeboy Industries he had managed to "metamorphosize" himself. Then he told them that means "change."

One day he came to work and plunked himself down in my office. "Last night, I was walkin' home from King Taco," he said. "You know, on Soto. Anyways, before I get to my canton, I'm crossing in front of that tiny park. You know the one. I see an old man lying on a bench. He's either asleep or tryin' to sleep. There's a half-full forty on the ground in front of him and the old guy, well, he's shiverin' cuz it's cold. So you know my favorite sweater?" I nod yes, though I don't know what he's talking about. I don't want to derail him. "Well, I was wearin' it and I took it off and I laid it over this guy. He didn't wake or notice."

For a moment, Andres enters a sort of trance. And then suddenly he's shaken from it. "Hey, I'm not tellin' ya all this so you think I'm AAALLLLL that." He stops again to think, and some long-held emotional stirring comes to the surface, making it momentarily hard to get the next words out. "Nah, I'm tellin' ya all this cuz I know that bench." He gathers himself. "I been on that bench."

Later, Andres shared this story with his therapist, who taught him a new word. "She told me," he said, standing in front of my desk, "that I was a man of integrity." The ego found its place so that it could rest in union with another, on a familiar bench. Andres found his true height.

A short rope. A leaf.

CHAPTER SIX

"The Good Journey"

There are easily fifteen tour groups—large and small, from all over the world—that visit Homeboy Industries each week. A woman once sent me a YouTube clip of her tour, which she had recorded on her cell phone. The tour guide was Eric, a nineteen-year-old African American gang member who had been a trainee just shy of a year. The clip shows Eric speaking to the group in front of our employment services department, which helps homies find jobs after their time with us. Eric begins, "As Father Greg *always* says . . ." Now, when a homie starts a sentence this way, rest assured what follows will be something that I have never uttered in my life. Eric does not disappoint. ". . . it's not about work for the homie, it's about the homie working on himself."

I've been quoting Eric ever since.

We try to change the way we see and turn things around, to walk in the other direction. "Not everything that is faced can be changed," James Baldwin wrote, "but nothing can be changed until it is faced." The task at hand is not to change behavior but rather to see clearly. After all, God doesn't want anything "from" us, only "for" us. God won't be loving a homie more if he stops gang-banging. God only has this holy longing to free us from terror and anxiety. A by-product of knowing this is behavior change. Then God's vision becomes ours. "When we see clearly," says Buddhist teacher Sylvia Boorstein, "we behave impeccably."

One night I swoop up three homies who I've heard are carousing in the Aliso Village housing project. It's nearing eight o'clock, and I know that if they willingly get in my car, I can drop them at their homes, avoiding the likely trouble they'll get into if left to their own devices. The best way to get them to cooperate, I've learned, is to feed them.

"Take us to Jack in the Crack," a homie might say.

"*Chale*, McNalgas" (McDonald's) another will groan in disagreement. I have no idea why they disparage both places; they are the only places homies ever want to go. I usually choose the eatery based on some interior calculation of the gang they are from and the relative level of "knuckleheadosity" they each exhibit. Tonight, Jack's it'll be, on Cesar Chavez and Mott.

As we stop at a traffic light, we hear someone speaking loudly into a megaphone about the benefits of following Jesus. On the corner, I see folks who look like they have "been there," former gang members and drug addicts, perhaps, preaching and handing out flyers. One of my passengers, Rusty, a personable seventeen-year-old, rolls down the window and grabs one from a large mustachioed guy as the light turns green. As we drive away, the sound of the megaphone fading, Rusty begins to read the flyer aloud, with a lot of effort. You could drive not just a truck but an entire fleet through the space between each word.

"Are you sick and tired? There is a way out." He slowly reads on. "Are you getting high? Do you gangbang? Do you drink too much? Are you depressed? Is your marriage failing?" He stops reading and places the sheet on his lap, eyes wide with realization. "Damn, G. Three outta five!"

———

"Working on yourself" doesn't move the dial on God's love. After all, that is already fixed at its highest setting. But the work one does seeks to align our lives with God's longing for us—that we be happy, joyful, and liberated from all that prevents us from seeing ourselves as God does.

I'm in my office talking to a homie, a senior staff member, when I catch a glimpse of Froggy in the reception area. Froggy is a seventeen-year-old who had worked for us for a time but was sent to a "suitable placement"—in his case, a group home—for a year after violating his probation. I wave to him and share my excitement with the homie seated there that he's been granted a pass to visit.

"Pass, my ass," the homie says and sighs. "He AWOL'd."

Immediately, I tell him to Bring Me the Head of Froggy. I prepare myself for a pointed conversation, in which I'll underscore that AWOLing is a big mistake, but that it can be corrected if he lets me drive him back to the group home before his Great Escape lands him on *America's Most Wanted*.

Froggy walks in. Or, rather, slinks in, shoulders slumped, no hug or greeting, like Charlie Brown after his kite gets stuck in a tree.

"Froggy, my son," I tell him, "I have three words for you," preparing to hand him a piece of paper on which I've written the word "mistake" three times. But he waves me off.

"I already be knowin' what the three words are," he says. I ask him, intrigued. Using his fingers to count them off, he recites, "Knuck . . . El . . . Head."

"All right," I tell him, "your three beat mine," and I throw my piece of paper away.

Some days, the best you can hope for is to plant yourself in the surety of a love that won't budge in the face of a knucklehead mistake.

On our last day before the Christmas break, Valentino, one of Homeboy's bakers, plunks himself down in my office. I ask him about his plans for the holiday, knowing that homies don't generally have homes to go to or large or extended families with whom they can celebrate.

"Well," he says, sighing some, "we gotta first go see the movie my lady wants to see, then later we'll see the movie I want to see."

"What's her movie?" I ask.

"*American Sniper*."

I laugh, as does Valentino.

"Yeah, well, you know *females*," he says. "They got to get them some romance." He air-quotes the last word, which makes me laugh again.

"What's your movie?" I ask.

"The new *Hobbit*." I ask if he has seen the others, and he says yes. "I love a movie with a good story," he says. Then he pauses, seeking more precision. "I love a movie with a good journey."

As they embark on the journey to turn their lives around, homies become accustomed to speaking of paths. "I used to walk the bad path," one might say, "but now I'm on the good path." It's a natural thing to say, but I don't think there are two paths. There is only the Good Journey. We are never on any other path but that one. There are obstacles along the way of the Good Journey, of course: ruts and gulches and seemingly insurmountable impasses requiring logs laid across the ravine over which we gingerly walk. At times we get stuck in mud or even quicksand on this path, but it is one journey and it is good inasmuch as it beckons us toward the God who calls us, who only wants us to be drawn forward. Homies begin to inhabit their truest selves once they are on the receiving end of tenderness. This, they soon discover, is its own reward.

I'm waiting for Lefty, summoned for confession, to come to our makeshift chapel at Camp Holton, another of the county's juvenile camps where I say mass. The altar has been set up in the TV room, just off the area where they lock down the most uncooperative residents. He arrives later than I would have liked, but he is quick to explain why: "I was walkin' across the field. Everybody's at rec time, but this one *vato* who is always looking for a beef with me stood right in front of me. He called me *leva*, *chavala*, lame. The crowd circled around us because they wanted us to fight. I told the guy I wasn't gonna fight him. I told him I was going to make my First Communion today. So I put my hand out to him and I said, 'Peace be with you.' And damn . . . he shook my hand back."

Christianity in its earliest years was known as "the Way"— not necessarily a secret formula but a path of transformation that would lead to abundant life. It was not an entry gate to how God might like us better but a good journey promising fullness.

Beto and I are standing in the Homeboy Bakery parking lot. His white uniform is covered in stains and dough and whatnot, bearing silent witness to the end of his long work day.

"Finally," Beto tells me, somewhat out of the blue, "I have brought honor to my father." He goes on to tell me how, in the past, his father would gather with his friends on a Saturday, and when they'd ask where Beto was, he would often have to say that he was in jail. "But now," Beto brightens, "he looks forward to gathering with this *bola* of his *camaradas*. He waits for the question, just so he can say, 'Beto is a baker.'"

And they say to Jesus: "Give us this bread always." And Jesus says, "Sure, I can do that." Fullness, light, happiness, and peace. The abundance promised.

It's easily two hours before he needs to be at work, yet Milton, just eighteen, leaps into my office. It's too early in the day to have this much enthusiasm. "I think I'm a rehabilitated gang member," he says excitedly.

"Do tell," I say as I sip my coffee.

"Well, there I am on the bus today, sitting next to a rich guy." (And I'm thinking, *How many rich guys in Los Angeles take the bus?* But I let him continue.) "He gots this cell phone. A bomb-ass, expensive cell phone. And I'm scopin' it out. And I think, damn, my old self would wait for the next stop, grab that shit, and run off the bus. The guy sees me admiring his phone, and just like that, he hands it to me. I couldn't believe it. He just *handed* me his cell phone."

"What did you do?" I ask, realizing that I'm leaning forward in my chair, fascinated.

"I checked it out, handed it back, and said, 'Let me give you some advice. Don't hand your stuff to strangers. You don't know who they are. My old self woulda run off this bus with your phone. But now I'm a rehabilitated gang member, cuz I work at Homeboy Industries.'"

Witness if you will this palpable joy, what Martin Luther King Jr. called "the power of God transforming the fatigue of despair into the buoyancy of hope." A thrill of hope, a weary homie rejoices. The "old self" is not defined by its bad behavior. Yet there is some unfamiliarity with the truth of dignity and thorough goodness. The "new self" . . . just needs to get up to speed.

A homie, quite proud of his personal transformation, once said to me: "I used to look in the mirror and say, 'You are a fuckup.' Now I say, 'I'm proud of you.'" He continued: "You see, G, I'm like an oyster. All this crap and dirt and sand gets in here"—patting his chest—"but it's just toughened me and protected me. Now look what I got. I got me a pearl"—he gently held his hand to his heart—"right here."

When Ignatius speaks of consolation, he means any movement that propels us in the forward direction. Desolation, then, is its opposite: not just feeling bad but also being kept from allowing our hearts to be cradled in God's. A homie, generally unable to filter his thoughts, met a stranger who had no legs. Unable to hold back, he looked at him and said, "Whoa. How do you manage?"

The legless man shrugged and said, "I just keep moving."

Pretty much it.

We keep moving, walking forward on the Good Journey, finding moments of joy along the way until those moments join together and usher in a life of happiness. So what we focus on and hope for, in the meantime, is a commitment to abide fully in our complete humanity. We bring as much compassion and wakefulness to our own lived experience and know that nothing human is ever abhorrent to God.

A homie, Shaggy, once texted me: "The curious paradox is that when I accept myself just as I am, then I can change."

I hadn't seen Adolfo in many years. He was eleven when we first bumped into each other. As he sat in my office as an adult, I asked how old he was. Initially, he was too embarrassed to tell me, but finally, with his eyes unable to meet mine, he muttered, "Forty-one." It had been thirty years since I first met this *travieso* kicking it with his homies. Now I realized he was mortified that in the intervening years he had not, in his mind, made much of himself. He felt, deeply, the disappointment at not having measured up. I told him simply that it was a privilege to know him and to have him gracefully returned to my life. Like the homie who presents to me some certificate of achievement for one thing or another, I want him to know that *he* is the achievement. Without that emphasis, one is left only with the sadness of years spent "not amounting to much." Adolfo was already the accomplishment. He just didn't know this yet.

As we look forward down the path, much sorting and sifting needs to happen before we can see clearly. Sometimes all we need is a new lens through which we must view the world. In Alcoholics Anonymous, there is a process called "taking inventory," which is about coming to terms with the damage we've done and identifying the thinking that always lands us in trouble.

During CPR training, Janet, a very butch homegirl, alarmingly tattooed, is asked to shake and scream at the dummy, the prelude to mouth-to-mouth. When it is her turn, instead of shaking and shouting at the dummy, she rifles through its pockets. The instructor asks what she's doing. "I think robbing her will wake her ass up faster than screamin' at her," Janet says. Moving beyond the mind you have is challenging. But if homies don't "come to terms," then they stay stuck in this sort of tunnel vision and never really get around to transformation.

That is why, at Homeboy, virtually everyone—our case managers, our peer navigators, and all positions in between—learn to hold folks and allow themselves to be held, reminding each other of their strength-based gifts that have the power to help us all conquer our fear that we cannot move forward. Jesus, after all, just sought to create relationships with the marginalized. How else, except through connection, can people be reminded of their goodness?

After I tell Carlos to enroll in the anger management classes we offer, he says, "Damn, G, I've taken anger management, like, ten times before and I still get mad." At HBI, we don't teach homies *not to be* angry but *how to be* angry. To move forward, homies must make a choice to no longer be a victim of their own anger. They befriend their wound to keep them from despising their wounded-ness. "Keep your loneliness warm," Thich Nhat Hanh tells us. Our brokenness is meant to be kept close.

Kendric, an African American gang member in his early thirties, comes into my office, having made a discovery. When he was nine years old, he tells me, his mom entered the living room where he was watching TV. She stood there with her arms outstretched. Kendric looked closer and saw that she had deeply slashed both of her wrists. Blood cascaded to the floor. "See what you made me do?" she said to him calmly, almost coldly.

The next day, Kendric was in foster care, and he remained there until he was seventeen. (His other two siblings, inexplicably, were never placed in the system.) At fourteen he was jumped into a gang. From the age of seventeen he was raised, from then on, in the prison system. Now, sitting in my office, this tough guy has been reduced to great sobs, all because of this single memory.

"I realized that I had preferred my rage over my shame," he says. This discovery, on the good journey, finally allowed him to forgive his mother for her mental illness and to forgive himself for having once been a nine-year-old boy. "The walking back," poet Jack Gilbert wrote, "was the arriving."

Often enough, folks will say that "one door closes and another door opens," but sometimes there is a hallway, a grace period before people find the next door. At Homeboy Industries, I tell our senior staff that part of our task is to "line the hallway," to make that distance stretching between the old and new versions of one's self a comforting one. We encourage and cajole with a constant tenderness as the tentative soul takes steps toward the fullness of becoming. The hallway can be long and the lure to return to an old, tired, but known and safe version can be compelling. And those who line the hallway haven't arrived fully either. Our mutual accompaniment with each other along the way pulls us all over the finish line. It's about the "rehab of the soul," as one of our senior staff puts it. We all line the hallway on this good journey with only gentleness in our rucksack and our own brokenness within reach.

I run into Joey at a Target. He's pushing a shopping cart and his two young boys are clinging to the sides, enjoying the ride, limber as two marsupials. We are happy to have this "aisle five" encounter. It's been a while. When he first came to us, Joey had been living in the heart of his enemy's neighborhood, fearful for his life and the constant pull of his homies. He became a trainee at Homeboy, and after eighteen months the job developers located a good-paying job for him in a warehouse. In the time since, he moved to a place where he could breathe easier. "That last place I lived," he says to me, "I'd be singin' the *Mission Impossible* theme song to myself as I ran to the bus stop. Now where I live, it's *calmado*. I be singin' '*It's a beautiful day in the neighborhood*.'"

Chance meetings like this in a Target give me an opportunity to take a homie's temperature, to gauge his commitment to his new life. I ask if he's heard from anyone from his "neighborhood" (his gang).

He shakes his head with something of a scowl and says no. "I don't go to the barrio. Don't hear from anyone anymore." Then something sparks a memory. "Well, wait . . . I did get a call a couple months ago from a youngster from the neighborhood. Don't know how he got my number. He called to say there was gonna be a meeting."

Gangs will, on occasion, meet in a park or any large venue to accommodate a hefty number of folks. Attendance is mandatory.

I asked how he responded. "I said, 'I'm not goin' to your meeting. I'm a man. I have a job. I'm a husband and a father. I'm not goin' to yer damn meeting." His tone in the telling is rock solid, and he even scoffs a little. I'm impressed. I ask what the response was. Joey shrugs with amusement.

"He called me a punk." In gang parlance, that's a tough word to be on the receiving end of. "I told him if I was a punk," Joey chuckles as he continues, "I'd be goin' to your meeting." As they say on game shows: "Good answer!"

The hope, always, is that homies won't settle for just answers but instead hold out for meaning. The goal is not perfection but a wholeness anchored in grateful living, in knowing what you have. Joey discovered that once you try wanting what you have, everything changes. The Peruvian priest Gustavo Gutiérrez believed that only one kind of person transforms the world: the one with the grateful heart.

A staff member ran into Speedy, a thoroughly active gang member back in the day who has now returned from prison and hit the streets a new man. "So how'd he seem?" I ask her.

"Well, you see Speedy has found Jesus," she begins, "and he's got him in a stranglehold. Jesus is turning blue, poor thing." As my ninety-two-year-old mother would say, "I'm all for it." Coming to terms with your life, however, is always more than replacing one addiction with another. Jesus points us beyond "the stranglehold" to a true awakening of the heart.

I was asked once during a Q and A in Australia, "When do you introduce Christ to the gang member?" I found myself saying, "Never, and immediately." The second any of us engage and enter into relationship with those on the margins, the Christ encounter is alive and well. After all, I don't bring gang members to Christ, I always say. They bring me to Christ.

At Homeboy, our goal is to offer a kind of resilience that can only come from relational engagement. This resilience is always anchored in the truth. Jesus speaks of those "who belong to the truth." It is not something you say but something you own. You belong to it. It is rooted in self-acceptance and openhearted awareness. The essential healing gang members find at Homeboy is truly nestled in the truth of who they are. Once you belong to that, a return to prison becomes inconceivable.

Curly rarely asks to talk to me, though he's been with us for six months. I had met him in a probation camp when he was younger, but now he's nineteen years old, graduated from our school, and just enrolled in community college. He's quiet, and English is still a struggle for him, his accent layering his words. But he does not often stand outside my door, wanting an "audience" with me, so I'm eager to usher him in.

"What's up, son?"

He tells me that he's learned something important. "I discovered that you are my father," he says. "Yeah. It's nice to have a father." He smiles slightly.

"Wow, dog," I tell him. "You just made my whole damn day. Imagine my pride if God had handed you to me and said, 'Here's your son, Curly.'" I pause for a moment, knowing the question I have to ask. "And your dad?"

Curly shakes his head. "He was never really there for me. Haven't seen him in, like, ten years." Then he drifts away for a moment, to the place all homies go when they talk about their pasts; after all these years, I can always tell. It's almost like a living photo album where they retrieve a snapshot they've tried to keep hidden. "My dad broke my arm once."

He tells me that his father came home from work one day, flying past Curly and his siblings, who were playing in the living room, to go to his bedroom. Within minutes he reemerged, furious, asking who had stolen his batteries. Well, little Curly had a toy requiring two batteries, and had found them in his father's dresser drawer. He tentatively raised his finger and said, "I did." His father walked over to him, grabbed his arm, and snapped it in two. "I was six years old," he manages to say through his sobs. He does the best he can to compose himself. "Yeah, it's nice finally to have a father." Even an initial embrace of one's own suffering will land on a spiritual intimacy with yourself and others that is utterly reliable.

Supervisors at our various social enterprises will call me and say, "You know that guy who you sent to us the other day? Well, he doesn't want to be here."

"Where is he right now?" I'll ask in response.

"Here," they'll say.

"Here" is as good a place to begin as any. Homeboy is like an AA meeting. Who's there? Someone twenty years sober; someone twenty minutes sober; and someone who's drunk . . . but he's there.

Lalo landed at Homeboy young, with decidedly only one foot in the door. The navigators, all homies who act as mentors of sorts, would need to "ear hustle" around Lalo in particular, since his banter, laced with gang-centric braggadocio, that we try to minimize, would wander into the provocative.

One of the classes he had agreed to attend was the Monday morning meditation class. Father Mark, who ran it, would shake his head at Lalo as he texted or talked during the quiet periods, distracting others. Mark tried to ignore him, hitting the gong and breathing in deeply. Then one day it just changed. Lalo began to breathe as deeply and as placidly as any Zen master. Four months into his time with us, he dropped by my office to tell me if it weren't for Homeboy he'd be dead. "Not locked up," he is determined to emphasize. "Dead."

One Friday he bumps into Father Mark in the hallway and asks if meditation is still scheduled for the coming Monday.

"Yeah," Mark assures him. "In fact," he adds, "I can see you leading the group." Lalo's face suddenly turns stricken.

"LEAVING the group?"

Folks on the margins are more than a little accustomed to being asked to leave a group. But leading one? Not so much. Lalo had learned, despite the stumbles along the way, that he didn't have to measure up to an abstract, unattainable idea of a better self. He just needed to show up and belong to his truth. He surrendered to it.

———

A criticism often leveled at me is that I "coddle" gang members. I'm not entirely sure what folks mean by this or what the alternative would be. Some people prefer "rigorous rehabilitation" because they fear "coddling." But it mainly means that they don't understand "awe" and are unable to see the degree of difficulty homies have in navigating their lives and history. All of us at Homeboy Industries are trying to help homies and homegirls do just that. To that end, we try to foster an irresistible culture of tenderness. We want this steady, harmonizing love to infiltrate the whole place. We often say to the homies: "We got you" (with a finger pointing) and "We got you" (with an open-armed *abrazo*). I am indeed heartened that gang members can receive, by and large, the occasional critique I send their way and not have them interpret it in any way other than loving, even if it's hard to take.

One time I correct Victor, a baker, about something and he does not take it well. He gives me oversized, sad dog eyes.

"Damn, G—you just made my self-esteem go lower than a lizard's nuts."

(I think the above story actually belongs in a chapter on "Manipulation.")

Sometimes a homie wants any other exit route than the one they desperately need to take. In the much-repeated pleading to get a homie into rehab, they will always say, "I have too much to lose." I will always tell them: "No . . . you have everything to gain."

Beaver, a heroin addict, fresh out of detox and now back on the streets, thinks he needs everything else but rehab. "'Sides, I got the rabbit in me," he says. "I'm gonna run." Then he shifts the subject. "You know what I need? I need to get my GED." He pauses.

"The Good Journey"

"What's 'GED' stand for anyway?" I write it out on a piece of paper. Then, on another slip of paper, I write "GYAIR." I hand it to him. Beaver studies the letters. "What's that stand for?"

"Get Your Ass Into Rehab."

When I celebrate masses in detention facilities, I remind folks before receiving the Eucharist that, as human beings, we often don't always get things right. So I welcome them to the human race, the whole catastrophe, in all our imperfection, so that they will come to communion. I have taken, lately, to loosely quoting Pope Francis, who says that communion is not some grand prize for the perfect person but rather food for the hungry one. When the time comes, I try to get the congregation to embrace their collective hunger and to have a lighter grasp on perfection.

Peeling our fingers from around perfection's throat, we can gain access to our worth and breathe easier at our human proclivity to get things wrong. "It's not about perfection," a lifer at Mule Creek State Prison told me once. "We shot that in the foot a long time ago."

Leo and Angel take the train with me to speak to a ballroom filled with psychologists at the Hotel del Coronado, made famous by the film *Some Like It Hot*. They each give the crowd a glimpse of their lives and help answer questions after our presentations. When we return to my office, the room fills with coworkers wanting to know how it went.

"They loved us," Leo begins, "and when we finished they gave us a stand-up probation." The office erupts into laughter and Leo turns to me, confused. "Standing ovation," I tell him. I expect him to be embarrassed by his mistake, but the laughter doesn't seem to rattle him. He's in a place where getting it perfectly right is not the coin of the realm. Worth beyond perfection, shot in the foot long ago.

This is why I generally don't give communion on the tongue,

as other priests might. Jesus handed the disciples the bread and they received it in the hand. And if he didn't give communion on the tongue, why should I? The underlying mentality and spirituality is wanting. (Besides, it's gross.) Once a very elegant woman attended a wedding at Dolores Mission. At communion, she stuck out her tongue expectantly. In these situations, I always say in Spanish, "It's better in the hand." But this woman, dressed to the nines, replied that she couldn't do as I said. I asked her why not, right there in the communion line. "*Soy sucia*" ("I'm dirty"). Her eyes brimmed with tears. I touched her arm and told her that God thinks she's magnificent. After a moment she took communion in the hand. God is not waiting around for us to prove our worthiness.

In the course of their good journey, homies often need to re-claim a childhood they've been denied. The class we teach called Baby and Me is not just a chance for them to learn how to play with their kids; it's an opportunity to catch up on lost time. Every Fri-day morning at 9:30, our mental health team plans arts and crafts, games, and songs for the homies and their toddlers. Sometimes a volunteer pediatrician from General Hospital is present to answer questions. The large classroom is a joyous place for an hour, filled with finger painting and clay shaping. Any latecomer is serenaded with "Good morning to you, good morning to you." There is a huge, brightly colored parachute laid out on the ground and a kid is placed in the middle and the homies gather round, take hold, and, in unison, toss the kid in the air. (I'm guessing this can't be safe.) The bright, shining faces belong to the homies as much as to the toddlers.

A new hire, Lica, a huge guy, two weeks out of prison, wanders into Baby and Me one morning. He sees the joyous goings-on, spots Theresa from our counseling staff, and breathlessly asks her if he can sign up for the class. She starts to write down his name. "Do ya gotta have a kid to be in it?" he asked. (Well . . . that's sort of the idea.) No one doubts that Lica once was a child, but it may be a safe bet that he had been denied a childhood. It turns out, you can get back what you've lost.

———————

I don't like doing panels. Like a house cleaner who "doesn't do windows," I find them largely a waste of time and usually a reflection of the event organizer's insecurity: you multiply the number of speakers, since you don't know if any one of them is good enough to carry the day. One time I was on a panel of thirty people. I spoke for exactly two minutes. I'll never get those two hours back. Though I try to avoid these setups, I will agree to participate in such an event if homies are invited to join me.

At one in particular, two homies join the usual suspects, the animal-vegetable-mineral of the gang issue: cops, academics, electeds. We're in a senior center, in front of the oldest crowd I have ever addressed. We sit on the stage, at tables lined with pitchers of water, glasses, and pristine notepads and pens. Sitting next me is Arturo, a gang member in his early thirties with a history of heroin addiction and prison visits. He is good now, though terrified at speaking to this packed house. He does fine, making his way into the collective heart of this audience.

An hour and a half later, we're done. I stand and then glance at Arturo's notepad. He has four lines written there:

> *Your children love you.*
> *Take your time.*
> *Don't hold back.*
> *Maximum Capacity.*

I suspect that this last line has been taken from the fire marshal's warning, above the illuminated exit sign, cautioning about how many old people can be crammed into this space. But I am awestruck at the clarity and simplicity of his reminders. The unofficial

Homeboy slogan is taken from Richard Rohr, who says, "If we do not transform our pain, we will most assuredly transmit it." It's heartening to hear homies speak of this to their younger charges. I tell the older guys, the ones who run the place, that it's never about behavior, it's about identity—that versions of an old self have to die in order for a new, brilliant one to emerge and see the light.

I'll admit, there are some homies you look at and think to yourself, *Yeah, I'm not so sure this guy will ever be able to turn the ship around.* You don't admit this to anyone, though. You keep it to yourself and hope that everyone—anyone—can alter course. People always surprise you.

Johnny was such a kid. I met him when he was fifteen, but never in my office. He never wanted to be seen there. I'd catch him in the alley where his homies would gather; he was way tougher than someone his age ought to be. He had certainly "put in work" for his neighborhood, stuff that eventually landed him in juvenile hall, then probation camp, then Youth Authority, and finally prison. He walked out of there at twenty years old yet still refused to set foot into Homeboy.

But it takes what it takes. Johnny found himself tending to his mother, who was struck with pancreatic cancer. In the last six months of her life, I'd visit and watch how tenderly Johnny would attend to her every need, becoming the hospice point person and caring for her with such affection. When she died, I buried her. A week later Johnny walked into Homeboy Industries.

Four months into his stay with us as a trainee, he wanders into my office to talk. "What happened to me yesterday," he begins, "has never happened to me in my life." He tells me that he was riding the LA Metro Gold Line train, which he caught at the Chinatown station, heading east after his day's work. The car he was in was packed, yet he managed to secure a seat for himself. Standing in front of him, hanging on to the pole, was a gang member, a little older than Johnny, but with tattoos and *medio pedo* (a little bit drunk). Johnny was wearing a Homeboy T-shirt with the insignia and slogan "Jobs Not Jails" quite large over his chest. The homie, still a little wobbly, looked closely at the shirt, then at Johnny.

"You work there?" he asked.

Johnny, initially hesitant to engage the guy, nodded.

"It any good?" the guy fired back—not belligerent, just persistent.

Johnny shrugged. "Well, it's helped me. I don't think I'll ever go back to prison because of this place," tapping the front of his shirt as he said it. Then Johnny stood, feeling as the prophet Ezekiel did when he wrote that "the Spirit set me on my feet." He fished a clean piece of paper from his pocket and located a pen from another. He wrote down the Homeboy address. He tells me, "I couldn't believe I knew it by heart."

Johnny handed the note to the man. "Come see us," he said. "We'll help you."

The guy hanging on the pole studied the piece of paper. "Thank you," he quietly replied. The train arrived at its next stop, and the guy got off. Johnny reclaimed his seat and looked around the train.

"What happens next," he tells me, "has never happened to me in my whole life. Everyone on the train was lookin' at me. Everyone on the train was noddin' at me. Everyone on the train was smilin' at me." His lip trembles and a tear escapes. "And for the first time in my life . . . I felt admired."

There is a Chinese proverb, "The beginning of wisdom is to call things by their right name." We want to find the right name for what was done to us, for what turned us around, for what is happening to us now. We all want to find our maximum capacity. And when that desire is strong enough, we find the legs to walk us through the hallway, down the path, on the Good Journey. The walking back is the arriving.

CHAPTER SEVEN

"Good Guy"

So here I am, on *Dr. Phil*. I know, I know: What was I thinking? But Dr. Phil was kind enough to highlight Homeboy Industries and promote my book on his show, and though we'd been nervous about how they would focus the segment, we thought we were all on the same page. How bad could it be? I'm seated next to Dr. Phil as he introduces me.

"I want you to meet an amazing man," he begins. "He is the author of the number-one bestselling book, *Tattoos on the Heart*. He's also the founder of Homeboy Industries, the largest gang intervention program in the country. Please welcome Father Greg Boyle."

The audience, including some homeboys who accompanied me for the show's taping, applauds. Then, to my horror, I see that on Phil's side of the stage is a mahogany coffin resting atop a velvet-draped church truck. I turn and then see that, on my side, is a perfectly reconstructed jail cell, complete with bars, bed, sink, and toilet. They went to great expense for these two set pieces.

African American, Latino, and white teenage young men, all vaguely involved with gangs, are the focus of the show, and they are accompanied by their distraught single mothers. Each pair is brought out one at a time.

You can see where this is going. Phil grabs the first boy by the collar (figuratively speaking) and gives him a good shake. "Don't ya see where this choice is leadin' ya?" He points at the two set pieces. "Prison or death." He does the same with the second kid. By the third, I can no longer keep quiet.

"Every kid who joins a gang," I break it to Phil, "knows it will lead to death or prison." Phil actually listens. "They don't need more information. They are not awaiting some new data. They know it will lead to death or to prison. They just don't care that it will."

Years ago I went to give blood, which I did regularly. My dad always gave blood, and since he and I shared the blood type anyone can use, we would always make several trips each year to the Red Cross. One year, after running the usual tests, the guy at the blood bank, looking at my initial results, blanched and told me to go to see a doctor—and fast. I did, and the doc diagnosed mononucleosis and treated me for mono for a year. Turns out I had leukemia. (I think we can all agree that there is a difference between the two.)

A bad diagnosis is never neutral. It always puts you behind the eight ball. You have to play catch-up, and that wastes time, money, and resources. No treatment plan worth a damn was ever born of a bad diagnosis. Never. A good diagnosis is everything.

No hopeful kid has ever joined a gang. Never in the history of gangs, and never in the history of kids. Not once, not ever. Hopeful kids don't join gangs. Gang involvement is about a lethal absence of hope. No kid is seeking anything when he joins a gang, he's always fleeing something. There are no exceptions. That is a good diagnosis.

Journalists in particular have a hard time with this concept. "Well, everyone *knows* that kids join gangs because they just want to belong," more than one has scoffed at me.

"Not true" is always my reply. "Kids join Little League because they want to belong. They join gangs because they want to die." I tell them that it's more accurate to report, "Everyone *says* kids join gangs because they want to belong." If they were to interview a homie, however, they would be told that the gang is like "a second family" and "they have my back." Gang members will say, essentially, they are looking for "wine, women and song." Join a gang— see the world. They say this because it is easier than explaining how "my mom used to put cigarettes out on me and hold my head in the toilet and flush until I nearly drowned." Gangs are the places kids go when they have realized their life as a misery. And who doesn't know by now that misery loves company? But in thirty years of walking with gang members, I've never met a bad guy. One would think I would have by now.

I am sixty-three years old and I've never killed another human being. If I asked you why that is, you might say it is because I know the difference between right and wrong. Or you might suggest that I have sufficient emotional intelligence not to let conflict spiral to such a murderous end. Both are true, but neither is relevant.

There are three great fortunes that have landed in my lap that account for the fact that I have never taken another person's life:

First: by sheer dumb luck, my life has been almost completely devoid of despair. I have always been able to imagine my future, and consequently I care about my life. (And because I do, I care about others' lives as well.)

Second, I cannot identify any defining trauma in my upbringing or in my life to date that would lead me to such a place of rage. Struggle and suffering, yes. But the *golpe* of huge, damaging trauma? Never.

Third, I have never been plagued by mental illness. I have never had to navigate schizophrenia or been burdened with sociopathy, psychopathy, or bipolarity. I have issues like everyone else, but I won the mental health lottery. It is not my moral superiority or heightened emotional intelligence that accounts for my lack of a murderous past. It is luck. Sheer dumb luck at that.

Every homie I know who has killed somebody—everyone—has carried a load one hundred times heavier than I have had to carry, weighed down by torture, violence, abuse, neglect, abandonment, or mental illness. Most of us have never borne that weight. We are free not to like that truth, but we are not free to deny it.

I take two homies, Spider and Mugsy, with me to speak to a gym full of high school students in Palm Desert. Both men are in their mid-thirties, are tattooed, and have seen most of their adult lives spread between drug addiction, gang violence, and incarceration.

"Decide right now not to romanticize any of your gang past," I tell them as we go inside. "Every homie who's ever come to terms with his life knows that no kid is seeking anything when he joins a gang; he's always fleeing something."

Spider goes first. He's exceedingly muscular and outwardly menacing, I suppose, until you chat with him and realize he's just a big ol' gentle giant, kind and soft-spoken. He begins by laying out the basics of his life's story, growing up in the projects, jumped into a gang very young, and dropping out of school. He stands on a makeshift stage facing bleachers full of rapt high schoolers. Somewhere early on in his telling, though, he stops. The silence is awkward and I don't know whether he's frozen or needs an assist. Just as I'm about to throw him a lifeline, he begins again.

"I think I was, like, five," he says. "Yeah, five. I was playin' with matches, you know, like kids do. Well, this pissed off my mom. So she grabbed me by the hand and dragged me into the kitchen. We had one a' them electrical coil stoves. So she turned it on high and waited till the coil was red-hot. Then she held my hand down on it for a long-ass time." The students gasp, and Spider tears up some. "All I remember," he continues, "was waking up asleep on the floor in the bathroom with my hand in the toilet water trying to get some relief, 'cause it was all burned and full of pus." Spider seems to enter into a state of deeper thought and heightened emotion. When he can finally speak, he points at his young audience. "That's why I joined a gang."

Nothing can render a person more a stranger to himself than the unspeakable things he was forced to endure when young. Coming to terms with the traumas of one's childhood is an arduous task. It's much easier not to look at it, and easier for everyone else not to hear of it.

I once heard a homie tell an audience that he joined a gang because he wanted "independence." And yet, there has never been a teenager who didn't want independence, so it was an innocuous and therefore an acceptable way to present his gang past. But his household was a nightmare. For him, it was easier to say he was seeking independence than to acknowledge his crackhead mom and the chaos of her drug-addled life. Once he'd even had to step over an addict's dead body in his living room as he made his way to school. Denial is perfectly beneficial until it's not anymore. Then we need to find the safe place to peel back the layers of our own pain.

———————

For all the years I had known Pedro, I couldn't recall a time that he ever mentioned his father. Keeping those memories distant was, perhaps, important to him, which was why I was surprised when suddenly, one day, he opened up.

"I walked in on my mom and dad," he said. "He was beating her badly. I was ten. I grabbed a big ol' stick and hit him over the head with it. It stunned him. I told him if he wanted to beat someone, he should beat me." He paused. "Well, I got my wish. He beat my ass."

I take Mauricio with me to speak to a psychology class at the University of California, Irvine. He's in his late thirties and quite visibly a gang member. After we finish our talk, a young woman in the class asks him why he ran away from home at nine years old, a fact he'd mentioned in his remarks.

Mauricio shrugs a little and says, "I was tired of listening to my parents."

Later, on the drive home, I ask him if he remembers what he'd said. He says yes. I ask him to repeat it.

"I said I ran away from home 'cause my mom would beat my ass."

I tell him that he said no such thing, that in fact he'd said he was tired of listening to his parents.

"*Serio?*" he says to me in disbelief. I ask him if he's ever met his father. No, he has not. His mother tortured him daily. One year, when he was in the second grade, she sent him to live in the backyard with a lengthy chain affixed around his neck. The yard became his toilet, his bedroom, his cell. Neighbors would sneak him food but never call the authorities on the mother. She finally let Mauricio back in the house once summer had ended. Running away from home two years later seemed pretty sensible.

A homie reminded me of something I once said in the "Thought for the Day," a portion of our daily morning meeting where we make announcements, celebrate birthdays, and pray to start the day.

"Find your story," he quoted me. "Know your story. Remember

your story. Tell your story. And always know, that at the end of your story, you are its hero." He said he had never forgotten that. I didn't recall having said it, but I took him at his word. "And here," he said, "I had always thought I was the villain of my story."

Good kids or bad kids. Gang members think they are the villains of their own stories largely because society has insisted on it. Finding the hero inside takes courageous and constant work. When I met Richard, he was serving time in the Youth Authority. I always just called him "Richard, the Heroic One." Not sure why I did. While he was with us at Homeboy, his wounds were still very fresh, and so the process of healing was incredibly painful.

One day I asked him how therapy was going. "It doesn't do any good," he replied. "I stopped going."

I looked at his tattoos, which I knew he was in the process of removing. "How many treatments have you gotten on those tattoos on your face?" I asked.

"Three," he said. "It takes a while 'cause it's dark ink."

I put my arm around him. "Richard, the Heroic One. You got dark ink inside here," I said, tapping his chest. "Be patient. It takes time."

A homegirl wrote to me from jail, "Every day, in my cell, I pray my demons won't come out of hiding." The things that haunt us, that cause us grief, can lead to emotional bludgeoning and tidal waves of shame. One of the signature marks of our God is the lifting of shame. Demons keep us from who we are. Jesus, we're told, drives out demons—or anything that's taken us over: drugs, *celos*, barrio. Yet, Jesus wants to demote "sinful behavior" and emphasize restoration in its place. Jesus, frankly, is not big on demons. He is more interested in driving out demonizing.

So people in bondage need liberation, and people in exile need to return home. People who are blind need to see, while people who are sick and wounded need healing. People who are outcast need community. But we have been programmed to think that sins define us and that, once we have reached that point, there is no going back. Homies have their behavior always on their minds. Their "sin" is the power pack driving their shame. This source of disgrace is never-ending, and they are aware that others identify them by it.

In the gospel of Luke, Jesus is passing through Jericho. He's not staying. The gospel writer seems determined to underscore this. Jesus is just passing through the town. The crowds gather to watch him pass. A villager named Zacchaeus is too small to see much, so he scrambles up a tree to catch sight of Jesus. As Jesus is passing through, he spots Zacchaeus and says that he wants to stay—at his house. The entire crowd gasps. Zacchaeus is the chief tax collector—that is, the poster child of "the bad guy," the most despised and demonized man of the time. Above all, Jesus wants to drive out demonizing. He seems to say to the horrified, gasping crowd, "There are no bad guys. Quit saying that there are."

I've known Eddie for thirty years. He's probably nearing fifty. He goes to mass at Dolores Mission every day with his father, Ramón, who is the church's faithful sacristan. He doesn't say much. Maybe he'll say, "Hug, hug, hug" before he gives you an *abrazo* during the Sign of Peace at mass. Often, he'll simply say, "Good guy" when he is standing in your presence. Sometimes, if you're particularly lucky that day, he'll say, "You're a good guy. You're a good guy."

There are no monsters, villains, or bad guys. Eddie seems to know this. There are only folks who carry unspeakable pain. There are among us the profoundly traumatized who deal in the currency of damage. And there are those whose minds are ill, whose sickness chases them every day. But there are no bad guys. Jesus seems to suggest that there are no exceptions to this. Yet it's hard for us to believe him.

At her sentencing to life without the possibility of parole, a young woman states simply: "I did what they say I did, but I'm not who they say I am."

———

Wayne LaPierre, the CEO for the NRA, has taken to saying, "The only thing that stops a bad guy with a gun is a good guy with a gun."

I gave a talk once in Sacramento, and afterward a man introduced himself to me by saying: "I represent the good guys." Eventually he revealed he was a lobbyist for the sheriffs in California. Since he had just sat through my keynote talk, I suppose he thought I represented the "bad guys."

When reporters do ride-alongs with cops on patrol for print and television stories, they will always ask their subjects what their mission is. Rarely do the cops say what is printed on their squad cars: "to protect and to serve." With an utter sameness, they will often say, "Our job is simple: get the bad guy." Or, as an officer once told me: "We're gonna crack down on the cream of the crud."

A few years ago, while driving back to the office from a speaking gig in Los Angeles, I turned on the radio to the news of an unfolding drama at LAX, where a TSA agent had just been tragically gunned down. The reporter was questioning an officer at the scene: "We understand that police have one bad guy in custody. Do officers feel that there are other bad guys out there?" This was NPR.

Once, after Dolores Mission had declared itself a sanctuary church not only for Central Americans fleeing war but also for the Mexican undocumented who didn't qualify for amnesty, I got a phone call. The caller said he had read in the *Los Angeles Times* of our church's commitment and that he deeply admired our principled stand. He asked for our address so he could send a donation. Pleasantries were exchanged until, suddenly, his voice dropped to some Beelzebub-like register and he said: "Now I'm going to tell you why I really called." He then unleashed a torrent of invective and racist obscenities so hateful that I finally hung up. The homie in my office at the time said that when the call ended, I looked whiter than I usually do.

Was this a close encounter of the "evil" kind? I used to say that it was. Now I am certain I was just speaking with a carrier of great pain. Desmond Tutu was right when he said there are no evil people, just evil acts; no monsters, just monstrous acts. A probation officer used to say, when certain homies would come up in conversation, "No use trying to help that guy. He's pure evil." Such comments merely compelled me to re-double my efforts. Slapping the dismissive label of "evil" on a person has never seemed very sophisticated or reverent of human complexity.

I only agree to testify as a gang expert in death penalty cases. This opportunity generally comes in the sentencing phase, and because I deeply oppose the death penalty, I often try to give a jury context to help them understand why the defendant became a gang member in the first place. You hope that some "There but for the grace of God . . ." kicks in for even one jury member so that a life is spared. Sometimes I've known the defendant, most times not.

Until we come to our senses and decide to stop executing people, I will continue to take the stand and do what I can. I've done this maybe fifty times; only twice have the defendants been sentenced to death. I'm asked by defense attorneys how much I charge for my testimony.

"Nothing," I tell them, "and be sure to ask me that on the stand." They usually do, and it allows me to state my opposition to the death penalty. This always sends both attorneys and the judge to holler and ask everyone in the courtroom to kindly ignore what has just been said. But even so, it hangs there in the air. And you hope it did some good.

Each prosecutor usually follows the same blueprint in their questioning. First, they establish that they like or respect me. Once, the prosecuting attorney began in this ambling, Andy Griffith–like way:

"Now Father, you seem like a nice guy. Kind, gentle. I mean, look at you." He flings his arm in my general direction. "You're Santa Claus."

There is silence in the court. I admit to having a white, full beard and that, yes, my poundage has probably gone to the North Pole in the last few years. But I turn to the judge and say, "Your Honor, I'd ask that the words, 'Santa' and 'Claus' be stricken from the record."

As soon as I said it, I regret it. This was an exacting judge who I know does not appreciate silliness. The court erupts in laughter and the jury is beside itself. But I only care about the guy in the black robe. I turn to the judge and see that he has folded his arms in front of himself. He rests his head there. I note that his shoulders are moving; we all have to wait until his giggling subsides. Rule number one in the death penalty sentencing phase: it's smooth sailing after your first laugh.

Next, I'm asked about choice. Wasn't the defendant free to choose whether or not to kill? Aren't we all free to choose our actions and then be responsible for those choices? I suppose, I begin. But I always remind the prosecution that not all choices are created equal. My decision not to join a gang as a teenager in Los Angeles can't be compared to the decision a kid growing up in public housing projects in LA faces; that choice was basically made for me. It was geography that mattered, not morality. The serendipitous lottery of zip codes.

Finally, we get to the question of "good" and "bad," "innocent" and "evil," which almost always gets presented in a litany of the heinous.

"What would you say, Father Boyle," the prosecutor begins, "about a man who . . ." And then he will present an unspeakable act in gruesome detail. Sometimes enlarged photos are exhibited.

"Well, gosh," I say, "imagine how bleak and dark one's despair would have to be to do such a thing."

The attorney continues, somewhat exasperated, with an even more grisly set of details.

"Imagine," I repeat, "how damaged and traumatized you'd have to be to do something so awful."

Blood pressure rising, the attorney unleashes the last horrific shot across the bow. He serves up the final, jaw-dropping, unimaginable set of events.

"I can't even fathom how mentally ill a person would have to be to do such a thing," I respond. This statement always causes the kerfuffle of all kerfuffles. The attorney, apoplectic at this point, will always ask if I am a psychiatrist.

"No," I say, "and neither are you. But no one needs to have taken Psych 101 for credit to recognize mental illness when they see it." Again the sheer mention of mental illness usually produces frothiness. The attorney slams his hand on the podium and points at me like we're in the "You can't handle the truth" scene with Jack Nicholson.

"You can't say 'evil,' can you?" he asks. My response is always the same.

"If I said 'evil,' I'd have to deny everything I know to be true about how complex human beings are. I'd have to embrace the least sophisticated take on crime and its roots to say that. So I can't."

The prosecutor walks over to the jury. He's in full disgust mode. He leans his arm on the edge of the jury box. He downshifts. "You preach on Sundays?" he asks, not looking at me.

"Yes," I say.

He laughs weirdly, then slams his hand down on the wood. "If you don't preach on evil, what *do* you preach on?"

I affect my most teenage voice crack. "Love?"

A second laugh from the jury doesn't hurt either.

A woman abducts a pregnant woman, stabs her, and carves out the fetus. The article reports that the police have come up with a motive: "She must have wanted a baby." Funny, I was gonna go with mental illness. Why is it so unacceptable to raise this as an answer to the horrific things we read about every day? The lead detective in the Robert Durst case says, "He's not crazy, he's diabolical." Still, he's bona fide, mentally unwell.

John Walsh, the host of the TV show *The Hunt with John Walsh*, is the best example of moral outrage inflated to the size of a Macy's Thanksgiving Day Parade balloon. One teaser for the show has a mug shot of a middle-aged white man while Walsh snarls with contempt, "What kind of man would shoot and kill his five-year-old daughter?" Well, I'm going to hit the buzzer marked "mentally ill," but that's not the answer he ever wants and neither do prosecutors in a death penalty case. They want to hear: "demon," "despicable," "less than human," "lowlife," "scum," and "evil."

I saw a sign in a probation camp once that read: "It IS your fault. You ARE accountable for your actions." The sentiment seems valid, except for the fact that it is wholly unsophisticated and not very helpful. It is a distinction, born of our own fear, that refuses to acknowledge the complexity of being human. It stands at a high moral distance and says, "*I* didn't join a gang. What's *your* problem?" If we could simply drop the burden of our own judgments, we could see with clarity and then compassion would be possible.

Moral outrage is the opposite of God; it only divides and separates what God wants for us, which is to be united in kinship. Moral outrage doesn't lead us to solutions—it keeps us from them. It keeps us from moving forward toward a fuller, more compassionate response to members of our community who belong to us, no matter what they've done.

And this is the most difficult part for us to grasp: because what could be more terrifying than actually believing that such folks belong to us? It requires a certain kind of identification that is harrowing for us to consider. But what if, for example, to the police there were no bad guys—only the desire to protect people? What if the only response was: we will not let you hurt yourself or anybody else. What if that shirtless old man in Miami, wielding a knife after an attempted bank robbery, was a member of our family, our "crazy Uncle Louie"? We know he's harmless, but because he had just established himself as a "bad guy"—noncompliant, knife, bank robbery—seven cops decided to fill him with bullets. No one is there to protect or speak for him. But if we had seen him as our Uncle Louie, there would have been a different outcome. What if, then, we insisted that everyone belonged to us? Everyone is our uncle Louie. No exceptions. "I am the other you. You are the other me." The invitation for the Christ in me is to see the Christ in you. There is no one outside of that way of seeing.

In the last few months, two guys have expressed the desire to kill me. The first guy declared it on Facebook: "I'm going to kill Fr. Greg." I don't really do Facebook, but the homies do and they were aware of the situation when the man came to Homeboy the day after the posting. They patted him down and one senior staff homie asked to sit in my office as he spoke to me. The young man was clearly troubled. Tenderness, however, seemed to carry the day and he left in peace.

The other came in with a gun, convinced his ex and I had done "witchcraft on his ass." In the middle of his visit with me, he stopped and listened to a voice only he could hear. I ended up walking him to the corner and giving him a blessing before he went on his way.

Years ago, on the front page of the morning paper, above the fold, was an article about a fifteen-year-old gang member who sat in a car outside of a courthouse, in a town east of Los Angeles, and shot and killed a California Highway Patrol officer as he left the building. The police apprehended him shortly after. It was reported that this kid admitted that he killed the officer "to impress his gang." I put the paper down, sipped my coffee, and said to myself, "Nope."

When I finally met the kid himself, while he was detained in the Youth Authority, it was clear that he indeed suffered from what anyone might call "mental illness." In the months ahead, at every detention facility I would visit, invariably I'd run into homies from the same neighborhood as this kid. Everyone would say the same thing. "That guy's not right in the head." "*Serio*, G. He's not all there." No one ever chooses to be tormented in this way. It was a daily terror that appeared at the door and refused to leave. "No one is born a slave," a homie named Cisco tells me, "but some of us are born into slavery."

Before a keynote I once gave, a sheriff from a large county spoke to the assembled crowd. He was mentioning a list of programs his department had begun to address the gang issue, which were intended to "help parents teach their kids how to make better choices." This stuck with me. When it was my turn to speak, I referenced the mother of James Holmes, the man who had shot and killed so many in a Colorado movie theater. During sentencing, she spoke movingly of her son from the stand:

"Schizophrenia chose him. He didn't choose it. And I still love my son."

Not all choices are created equal. When I toss this into my talk, I can see that one of the homies I've brought with me, seated at a table on the floor of the convention center, is crying. When I ask him about it later, he tells me that he realized, for the first time in his life, that he hadn't chosen the gang lifestyle; it had chosen him. Father, brothers, uncles, aunts, all killed by gang violence. "Yeah," he says, "it chose me."

A homie named Memo never knew his mom and dad and doesn't like to think about them, as it is too painful. After his parents died, he was raised by an aunt who was somewhat notorious in his neighborhood. She was killed when he was nine. He was once asked how old he was when he started gangbanging.

"In the womb," he said sadly.

Memo is always on the search for his roots, thinking one moment that he is Japanese and convinced another moment that he's Jewish. He greets me every day with "Mazel tov." In a morning meeting once, I mentioned that God's nickname for God's people in the Old Testament was "God's delight." For days, Memo would greet people this way: "Good morning, God's delight." And he took the concept straight to heart. When the father of Shirley, a member of our executive team, died, Memo consoled her by saying: "You know, if I was your dad and I was looking down from heaven at you, I would say, 'Mission accomplished.'"

One time I saw Memo on the second floor of Homeboy grasping at his heart and walking with some trepidation. "Are you having a heart attack?" I asked.

He clutched his chest and hesitated. "Low-key, yeah." Before I called for help, he clarified. "Actually, I think I'm having the opposite of a heart attack. Hey, G, what's the opposite of a heart attack?" I tell him I have no idea. "I'm feeling peaceful. Good. Happy. It's not a heart attack, it's a heart . . . peace." His hand gently rested on his chest. "Yeah, that's it. A heart peace." Who knows how, but Memo has landed someplace where what we think and believe becomes what we do and experience.

"I don't feel no ways tired," the gospel hymn goes, "I've come too far from where I started from. / Nobody told me that the road would be easy. / I don't believe He brought me this far to leave me."

I'm waiting on the C yard at Folsom Prison with "Al Bundy." The other inmates call him that not just because he is "married . . . with children" but because, apparently, he has twelve kids. His main prison job is to dole out athletic equipment to the other inmates. He is among the gentlest souls I have ever known. He is one of my teachers. He has learned "the tender gravity of kindness," in the

words of poet Naomi Shihab Nye, and knows, as well, "how desolate the landscape can be between the regions of kindness."

He and I both are waiting for the guards to "call yard." It's getting late. Three guards, their shifts having ended, leave the building and walk past us. Al reaches out to one of them and asks if he
has the time. He stops, as do the other two, and makes a big show
of looking at his watch. Then he says to Al, "It's about . . . time for
you to get a watch."

The three guards guffaw as they leave, but Al remains, feeling the sting of humiliation. I place my hand on his back. Another
brave-souled inmate, once the guards are out of earshot, says, "Why
didn't you tell him something? You shouldn't let him get away with
that." I look at Al, and you can see, right there, a transformation.
He refuses to cling to the pang of the insult and moves quickly to
clinging's opposite: cherishing.

"Naw, he's going home to his wife and kids," he says. "What if
I said something and got him mad? Maybe he'd go home and hit
his wife or beat his kids. Naw."

Loving as the ground of your being. Al Bundy always knew
how to locate the freedom to choose, habitually, the most loving
thing. His effort was never really about perfecting himself or becoming a "good" person. It was about making his already-good
love more perfect and real. Beyond the designations we have for
each other—felon, loser, bad guy—we are all just doing our best to
find ourselves connected to each other. Still, we must try and "lean
in past the labels," as Buddhist teaching instructs.

After a homie's transformation, his own choosing needs to be
constant. A "yes" must be repeated, deepened, made new over and
over again—or else it ultimately becomes a "no." In a vocation, a
marriage, recovery—no matter what your lips seem to be saying—
you have to renew this "yes" all the time. At Homeboy, we want
folks to constantly acquaint themselves with their natural fearless-
ness—what Martin Luther King called our "soul force." We don't

try to get them to be "good"; they already are. We're hoping they'll find the goodness and seek happiness in their "yes."

———————

At 7:30 in the morning, Abel, a sixteen-year-old gang member and trainee, is waiting in front of the Homeboy office. Ever since he read Celeste Fremon's *G-Dog and the Homeboys*, Abel wanted to have "Stah-mee-na," he told me, just like what was mentioned in the book. (It took me a long time to realize he meant "stamina.") So he's been getting up early, running a couple of miles, and getting to the office before anyone else. This morning, shifting around impatiently, Abel goes to the office door to check if someone, somehow, has unlocked it from the inside, just as cops from the anti-gang CRASH unit drive by. The cops make a U-turn and pull up alongside him.

"You fuckin' mad-doggin' us?" they yell at him from the car. Abel says he isn't. "You don't get to fuckin' mad-dog us," they yell again. "We're the police. What are you doin' here?"

"Waitin' for Father Greg to show up," Abel responds. "I work here."

"Father Greg ain't shit and neither is this place," they reply.

When we label folks scum, it makes it all right to do anything we want to them. Who doesn't belong? We try and imagine Jesus and God compiling a list of those who should not make the cut, but we come up short. We can't think of anybody. The minute we accept this to be true, we will see racism, demonizing, and scapegoating dissipate in the wind like sand on a blustery day. The great Jesuit Howard Gray said: "God has no enemies and neither should I."

———————

Once a day, a homie named Trayvon would walk the second floor of Homeboy's headquarters, clap his hands, and yell, "Stay focused, people." Those occupying the cubicles would poke their heads up like meerkats and this giddy silliness would slay them every time. Tray was twenty-eight years old and had spent considerable time in prison. He felt the usual gravitational "push" from a household devoid of healthy parenting toward drug abuse and violence. Watching Trayvon in action always left me wondering how he had managed to find ebullience and gentle humor in such a childhood, for he was surely fleeing a great deal when he sidled up to his gang. At Homeboy, he healed much of the racial strife that follows gang members out of prison, connecting former enemies and making them friends. This was no small feat. Having gang enemies is one thing; harboring mistrust of an entire race, quite another. Tray was this human suspension bridge giving everyone an ability to cross to the other side to a place of kinship.

I once took him, along with Miguel, on a trip to the San Francisco Bay Area. Flights from Los Angeles are brief, so it's a good way to expose uninitiated homies to air travel, and San Francisco offers a multitude of touristy things to keep them interested. From Alcatraz Island to the Golden Gate Bridge, even the toughest of homies are always aflutter with delight.

After a seafood dinner at Fisherman's Wharf, we head to Ghirardelli for the obligatory hot fudge sundae. Trayvon was always more loquacious than the average *vato*. He'd opine on any number of subjects. If I needed a clarification on something he'd said, he would often say, "G, pass the mustard and catch up." I loved that he'd be dismissive; it was always playful and clear.

As we sat there attacking these mammoth sundaes, a woman approached and asked if I was in fact Father Greg Boyle. She was there with her family and had heard me speak before. After the exchange, I feign that I'm bothered by the attention. "Well, so much for traveling incognito," I say with a shrug.

"Or, as my people call it," Tray says, stone-faced, "'in-cog-Negro.'"

The next day I was scheduled to deliver the closing keynote to some five hundred young adults who had committed to "Teach for America." Miguel and Trayvon were along for the ride and weren't going to speak to the group, but I acknowledged their presence as I began my talk. After I finished, the two men were swarmed by these young folks, mainly females. I watched as they held court, the women gripping every word that flowed from them. At some point, from across the room, I caught Trayvon's eye and pointed to my watch to indicate we had to leave.

As the three of us walked to our rental car, I said I was impressed by how interested the women had been in what they had to say. Tray responded quickly.

"Let's just say . . . we were reaping the benefits of your talk." But then he paused. "That made me feel important, right now."

"What did?" I asked.

"Well, I told those ladies that we had to leave, and when they asked why, I looked at them and said, 'Got a flight to catch.' I've never said those words in my life. Made my ass feel important. Then I said, 'We're catchin' the red-eye.'"

I gently told Tray that the "red-eye" was when you flew at night and arrived at your destination all "tore up" without sleep—you know, with red eyes. I reminded him that our flight was leaving at four in the afternoon.

"Damn," he says, "I probably shouldn't have said that, then." We climbed into the car. "Anyways," Tray added as he settled into his seat, "made my ass feel important."

Who knows what happened when Trayvon was gunned down at a picnic a few months later? Too many guns. Too much despondent darkness. If only we could "stay focused, people." In a packed funeral home in Inglewood, I told the mourners that Tray had a flight to catch.

Once a gang member, always a gang member. Once a felon, always a felon. Once a surly guard, always one. They are "the other" and most assuredly belong to Them and not to Us. They are "the monsters at the margins." But the truth is, we belong to each other, and to this spacious God of ours, who thinks there are no bad guys, just beloved children.

I take Kenneth and LeQuan to Washington, DC, in November to speak at Georgetown Prep, a private high school in North Bethesda, Maryland. In taking the homies on these trips, I hope to underscore that they are indeed the heroes of their own stories and that those stories matter. Kenneth was packing a suitcase for the trip, and his very young son asked where he was going. "On a business trip with my boss," Kenneth told him.

"The big, fat white guy with the white beard?" the boy asked. (Again, thank you very much.)

A few days later, the three of us stand on the steps in front of the Lincoln Memorial. Kenneth looks out over the reflecting pool stretching toward the Washington Monument and seems to suddenly realize where he is.

"Wow. *This* is the place," he says. I sense he was growing "verklempt." Then, suddenly, he yells out, to no one in particular: "Jen-ny!" After a moment, he answers his own cry: "For-rest!"

I was thinking, maybe, "I have a dream . . ." Not *Forrest Gump . . .*

Later, we walked to the Smithsonian Institution, thinly layered and ill-prepared for the freezing temperatures. Standing at a crosswalk and waiting for the signal to change, doing jigs to stay warm, LeQuan began to sing: *"It's the most wonderful tiiiime of the year."* Kenneth and I looked at him, stunned. Not exactly a tune from the hood (LeQuan lived for a long time in foster care with white folks) but it was nonetheless a perfect expression of what these two seemed to feel on the trip, buoyed by the standing ovation they received from a gym full of high school kids. Heroic in the telling of their stories and in their clear transcending of their stories' horrors.

Back at Homeboy, there was a homie named Nando who was adjusting to his new life. Straight out of probation camp at seventeen, he was a part-timer, clocking in and washing windows but avoiding any odious tasks, like cleaning the urinals. Camp kids have some adjusting to do when they first arrive at Homeboy. When you ask them their names, for instance, they will instinctively answer, "Martinez, Sergio," in this regimented "Sir, yes, sir" way. I tell them they never have to answer like that again. It's first names first here. Once a kid, right out of camp and only a handful of days with us, stood at attention in my office door and said, "Sir, permission to double-time it to do a sit-down." I reminded him that no one here needed expressed approval to use the bathroom.

Nando spent his mornings at our alternative school, Learning Works@Homeboy, arriving at 1:00 p.m. to begin work. One day there was a noticeable bounce in his being as he rushed into my office and sat in the chair in front of me. He flung a folded yellow card on my desk, worn and damp from so much human handling, the edges of the folds darkened with perspiration.

"I'm showin' this to everybody," he tells me. "I mean, I've never gotten a report card like this." I unfold the card carefully, like it's some historical artifact. The grades are unremarkable, but I try to echo his enthusiasm with a nod and a "Wow." My eyes can't help but move right to where it says he was late for school nine times and missed another five days during the marking period.

"I mean, never have I *ever* gotten a report card like this," Nando continues. "I'm showin' it to total strangers." He sports a broad and unwavering smile. My eyes move to the comments column. "Often disruptive" and "Talks too much" are among the critiques. I'm about to tell him not to miss school, don't be late, shut your pie hole.

But I can't do it. Something new is happening. Nando is showing up for his life and this is his certificate of merit. No villain in sight. No bad guy but only heroic plentitude. This report card is the badge of honor reminding him that his life is workable, that tenderness is possible, and that somehow hope is revived in this surprising buoyancy.

Yes, I tell him. Show every stranger you meet.

CHAPTER EIGHT

The Choir

In a recent magazine Q and A, Whoopi Goldberg was asked to name the living person she most admired. "Pope Francis," she responded. "Yeah," she added, ". . . he's goin' with the original program." When I mention this in my talks, the crowd always responds the same way: laughter and cheers. It's because people know what the "original program" is. They both recognize and connect to it. They get it.

People know that the "original program" is about living the gospel with joy and always being mindful of the poor. They know it is an invitation to the margins, knowing that if we stand there, the margins get erased. It's not about taking the right stand on issues but about standing in the right place, with the excluded and the demonized. When Jorge Mario Bergoglio was elected pope and took the name Francis, Cardinal Cláudio Hummes of Brazil gave him an *abrazo* and said, "Don't forget the poor." And indeed he hasn't.

As Pope Francis galvanizes our sense of the original program today, Pedro Arrupe did this for me when I entered the Jesuits in 1972. He was superior general of the Society of Jesus at the time and remained so until just before I was ordained. He was everything we young Jesuits aspired to be: simple, holy, and luminous. He had famously ministered to the victims of the bombing in Hiroshima. In the aftermath, he ran straight into the bomb's wreckage, only wanting to cast his lot with those facing unthinkable suffering. My generation emulated the same longing to run toward a bomb's aftermath, rather than in the other direction.

In the summer of 1976, I was community organizing in the Bronx with my good friend and Jesuit brother Kevin Ballard. When we heard that Pedro Arrupe was giving a speech in Philadelphia, we immediately commandeered a car, arriving at the event with fifteen minutes to spare. I had drunk a large amount of coffee over the course of the trip, so as soon as we parked the car, I asked for directions to the restroom. I found myself in some dimly lit basement and tried to follow what light was there. Then I saw him: Pedro Arrupe, standing by himself under a lightbulb, shining like the star on Christmas Eve. I walked toward him. He was radiant, exuding a sublime serenity that drew me to him. When I was within reach, he grabbed my hands like he had been waiting for me. I knew I was in the presence of someone who could read my heart and soul at first glance. He held my hands, looked me in the eyes, and said one word.

"Bathroom?"

I nodded like a *menso*. He pointed across the hall. And that . . . was the entirety of my Pedro Arrupe encounter.

"Anyways . . ." (as the homies say), years later, Pedro Arrupe was visiting Brazil when, by chance, he met a very poor man who invited him to his home in a nearby favela. He had a gift for the padre, he explained. So Arrupe accompanied the man and was led to a shack, where the man lived with his wife and children. It was so rough, small, and spare, it took Arrupe's breath away. He was moved so deeply, his eyes brimmed with tears. The man led him to a huge opening in the wall. Not a window but just a hole, and he pointed. It was a sunset. The only gift he could give was the view. "I know," Don Pedro later said, "that we learn much when we visit the poor." The view from there is what we get.

That pure, simple, loving outlook is why we, the Choir, are drawn to the original program. It's not a liberal or conservative view; it is a holy, radical take, precisely because it *takes* seriously what Jesus took seriously: inclusion, nonviolence, unconditionally compassionate loving-kindness, and acceptance. The Choir finds itself drawn like moths to the flame of its authenticity. What we discover when we embrace it is that true spirituality ought not end in the privacy of our soul but in real kinship with the poor. If we can find ourselves in this salvific relationship to those on the margins, we see as never before and it becomes our passageway.

The Choir, the people of God, finds its authentic courage when it can echo the words of Jesus: "Do not be afraid." A homie told me once that some version of that phrase is mentioned 365 times in the whole of Scripture. "One for every day of the year," he said. Another friend has a mantra, "Be fearless for me." He uses this often as a prayer to fill the empty spaces in the between times. Choosing to be fearless for the other awakens in us a courageous heart and fosters a selflessness where true joy is born.

Bear was a huge *vato* who came by his *placa*, or nickname, more for being kind and cuddly than a grizzly menace. He was much beloved and worshipped by the younger guys, which I never minded, because they admired that he was a husband, father, and a man of integrity, despite his earlier allegiance to his gang. He grew up in his barrio and later lived on the block, in his gang turf, with his wife and kids, having managed to step away from active gang life.

The neighborhood would get "hot" occasionally, but he refused to relocate. "I grew up here," he'd say, "It's my home—I'm not going anywhere." Few of us were completely surprised, then, when, while watering his front lawn early one evening after work, Bear was felled by a flurry of bullets from a passing car. He nearly lost his life and struggled in ICU for a time until he was finally placed in the hospital's step-down unit to recover.

One day, when I came to visit, I found two homies, Shorty and Magoo, standing vigil at Bear's bedside. Despite only a five-year age difference, they held Bear on a particularly high pedestal, a shining example of the man they wanted to become. A real man, they thought, looks like Bear.

Though there were tubes and monitors everywhere, I could see that Bear was out of danger. Having visited many homies over the years who were shot and in the hospital, I knew this scene. Shorty and Magoo, however, were beside themselves, convinced that this was the end. It didn't matter what I said or how I tried to calm them. They were overwhelmed, not only with the idea of Bear's mortality, but with the reminder of theirs as well.

Then Bear slowly opened his eyes. He smiled when he saw us.

"Magoo. Shorty. G," he said, his voice raspy. "Thanks for comin'." Even half-sedated, he must have caught a glimpse of these two homies' vise grip on dead seriousness, because a few minutes later he looked at Magoo. "Magoo," he said, with some labor. Magoo grabbed Bear's hand in the "homie grasp" in response, looking at his friend with intensity. Clearly, he thought that a final, deathbed request ("Raise my kids"; "Marry my wife") was about to be delivered. Magoo leaned in closer. So did Shorty.

"Magoo," Bear whispered again. "Did you, just now, put your hand under the sheets . . . and touch my dick?"

After a stunned pause, we howled with laughter.

Magoo released his hold on Bear's hand. "Fool," he muttered.

"It's okay if you did," Bear added. "Nothing to be ashamed of."

"Mutha-fucka," Magoo said as he took another step back, away from his deathbed earnestness, and laughing as he said it.

As we continue to laugh, I watched as Bear closed his eyes and returned to sleep, the unmistakable trace of a smile on his lips as he did so. Now I think to myself, *Mutha-fucka*. He was fearless for them. He saw the grip of terror holding these guys, and he reached in and untangled the knot as deftly and selflessly as I'd ever seen. His generosity dissolved all fear and let love fill the void. Let's build a cathedral on this spot.

———

One day, I overheard a homie who was giving a tour of our headquarters say to his group, "Here at Homeboy, we laugh from the stomach." This is no small thing. The laughter comes from the deepest place. Nothing fake or superficial. As the world has its occasionally grim realities to contend with and everyone carries more than their share of woes, laughing from the stomach ensures our survival. Homeboy Industries is held together, truly, by its humor, "self-defecating" and otherwise. It is how a community achieves a oneness as it holds folks through truly difficult times. Silliness, I have learned, has its place in the sacred and in the oneness of the Choir.

I have spent more time with gang members in my car than I can calculate, bringing them to appointments or to speeches, or just trying to keep them out of trouble. No trip happens without an abundance of *carcajadas*—side-splitting roars produced by unbridled silliness. Leaving a Jack in the Box once, the homies start to laugh uncontrollably, clutching their giant soda cups. A guy in the backseat gets on a coughing jag, a case of "wrong pipe" syndrome. A homie next to him begins to scream in a faux panic. "Call 411! Call 411!"

"Don't you mean 911?" I yell back.

"Well, then, call 411 and get the number for 911!"

More laughter-induced choking ensues.

As a church, as the Choir, we must stop at nothing to find our joy. Not in a ruthless, cutthroat way but in a way that is genuine and determined. We choose joy in all its constant delighting. After all, there is no group more practiced at fretting and worry than human beings. Delighting is a real antidote to the chronic toxic stress that folks at the edges carry.

A homie said to me once, "I've been shot at close range; been stabbed a gang a' times; been on life support, jumped, and beaten. If someone wants to come at me, bring it on. I don't give a fuck. I'm not even a little bit scared. Bring it on." He paused, slowly filling with emotion. "But put me in a room alone with a counselor and ask me about what happened to me as a child. That scares the fuck out of me. Then I'm just a little boy in a big-ass room."

In Luke's gospel, Jesus speaks of the coming of earthquakes, plagues, and famine, and then says, "Do not be terrified." And yet, it's not an assurance; it's an instruction. I'll teach you to see the terror as I do, he says, so we can get to the other side of what frightens us. When life throws a knife at us, we can either catch it by the blade or by the handle. We can stare right back at the terrifying darkness of what we've been through in our lives and grab it by the handle. We confront it with an open-hearted kindness as Jesus does. Suddenly, plagues and earthquakes have lost their menace when met with such tenderness.

I celebrate a *quinceañera* with two girls, cousins. At the end of the mass, the girls and their entourages leave as the mariachi plays. I recruit two other kids, a boy and a girl, to take the two frilly, heart-shaped pillows that the girls knelt on during the ceremony and walk out with them in the procession. They are about six years old. The girl grabs her pillow and demurely makes her way down the aisle. The boy, however, is beside himself with excitement, so thrilled to have been called into duty that he grabs the pillow and, before turning to leave, holds it up to me, beaming and smiling.

"This is the size of your heart!" he proclaims. And he turns and leaves, triumphant. I'm left startled by it—not just because, in truth, my heart is considerably smaller than this kid thinks, but because one so young could be so skilled at melting away who I am not. He pulled the beauty and favor right out of me, like a magician with a top hat and a bouquet of flowers. How'd he do that? To embrace tenderness, writes the theologian Jean Vanier, is the highest mark of spiritual maturity.

Another great Jesuit, Dean Brackley, who died too young, once spoke movingly of meeting his hero, Dorothy Day, when he was in his twenties and studying to be a priest. When he asked her how to live the gospel, she simply replied: "Stay close to the poor." She could have said, I suppose, help the poor, rescue the poor, save the poor. But no—stay close to the poor. The invitation is not to romanticize the poor but to recognize that some essential piece of our own salvation is tied up in our proximity to those on the outskirts. Jesuit theologian Jon Sobrino suggests as much in his provocatively titled book *No Salvation Outside the Poor*.

One of our tutors at Homeboy, Ms. June, is managing a roomful of students, whom she is teaching to fill out forms. She is a tiny Japanese American woman, a retired teacher who volunteers once a week helping homies on their literacy skills. One of the many homies she's working with is named Fili. When the form asks for his height, he doesn't know how to answer; confined to a wheelchair by gun violence, he is about three feet sitting upright. Ms. June asks him to extend his arms wide. She measures him from fingertip to fingertip.

"You're six feet tall," she tells him matter-of-factly. I, for one, never knew arm span equaled height. For our true height in love, it seems, is measured in how expansively we can outstretch our arms, with generosity and love. Sometimes there are lessons learned at the margins that can't be found elsewhere. It is where the Choir finds its true height.

An inmate on death row told me once that, despite his physical confinement and limited time, he had decided "not to be locked up" anymore. And I'll be damned, he wasn't. In fact, I have met plenty of inmates who left prison well before they were released from jail. I asked one how he managed it, and he told me that prayer was where he found his way. He knew, even from where he was sitting, that prayer should help us enter the world, not run from it. Staying close to the poor presents a whole new view.

The first funeral I ever did as a priest was in Bolivia. The deceased was a man named Luis and he was a campesino. He harvested flowers for the open-air market in the tiny mountaintop village of Tirani, where pretty much everybody was in the flower biz. I didn't know Luis or his wife, Maria, but I had sort of become the region's priest, mainly serving the community of Temporal, which was down the mountain and closer to Cochabamba. Like in most Latin American and poor places, if you die on Tuesday, you're buried on Wednesday. As Maria and I awaited the gravediggers to lower Luis into the ground after the other mourners had left, she began to sob inconsolably. I soon discovered that piled onto her grief and loss was a profound sense of shame and guilt. She and Luis had not been married, she revealed, "*por la Iglesia.*" And now it was too late. Right then, I opened my book to the marriage rite. The coffin had a window in it, so we could see Luis, looking exceedingly uncomfortable in a tie and an impossibly high, starched white collar. It was an outfit he might have worn at . . . well, his wedding. I asked Maria to put her hand on the glass. She repeated after me, "I, Maria, take you Luis." She could barely speak, the words were so soaked with emotion and tears. Then it came to the man's part. This was going to be a challenge.

The Choir

I don't know exactly how to describe what happened next. It was this side of Charlie McCarthy. I didn't exactly throw my voice, but lowered it to a whispering register as I stood as proxy for Luis.

"I, Luis, take you Maria . . ." I placed my hand gently on the glass window, as if the ritual instructed me to do so. Soon it was over and they were hitched (or I had inadvertently married myself to Maria). However it had happened, she was liberated, as surely as any character in the gospel. Show of hands: Does anyone here think God and/or Jesus would have had a problem with this ventriloquist's exchange of vows? Exactly. Original program.

I was told a story once about a homie riding the Gold Line train. Apparently, he looked fretful and anxious enough that an old black man got up and sat next to him.

"I can tell you're worried about something," he said kindly to him. The homie spoke to this stranger as he never had with anyone. All the sad moments, the disappointments, the shortcomings, to this person he had never met before. The old man's advice was simply this: "Stay close to your heart. You'll be okay." God is in every kindness.

The founder of academic medicine, William Osler, wrote, "I don't want to know the disease the person has. I want to know the person the disease has." It is, in essence, the difference between carrying the torch and being the torch. When we shine light, the darkness doesn't necessarily disappear. It doesn't seem to leave—that unspeakable thing that happened to you that reduces you to "a little boy in a big-ass room"—but now it merges with the light. The terrible thing has become bright. Not obliterated, but its own kind of fuel, its own kind of illumination.

Years ago, I would drive Pato, one of our bakers, home after his shift. He would take his leave the same way every time. He'd open the door, straddle between being in and out, and turn to me and say, "Today was a beautiful day. Tomorrow will be even better." Being the torch, fearlessly, allows you to say such a thing. The holiness of the Choir, then, is to be fearless for the other, to be unafraid to pull another soul out of the paralyzing grip of terror and assure them that all will be well. Jesus, after all, didn't co-sign on the disciples' terror when he entered that closed room after the Crucifixion. He opened the drapes and the windows and unlocked the door and said, "*Ándale.*" Let's go.

In John's gospel, Jesus says farewell and consoles us with "I will not leave you as orphans." "Orphan" is a word packed with meaning and significance, especially at Homeboy Industries, where virtually everyone there is one. Surely, the word finds much of its charge from the earliest biblical agreement between God and God's people. For this reason, like most utterances of Jesus in the Gospel, "I will not leave you as orphans" is not just supposed to fill us with consolation but to be received as an invitation. It seems to say, *As I won't leave you an orphan, don't* you *leave anyone behind.* We are meant to hear in these words a call to seek out the isolated, the rejected, the abandoned. Then we are meant to walk toward them, with open arms, and bring them in to the place of belonging. This is the essential task of the Choir.

I take two homies, Gabino and Israel, to Knoxville, Tennessee, to speak at the Children's Defense Fund's Haley Farm summer program. Gabino is, at the time, the tiniest worker at HBI. Quick-witted and nimble on his feet, he always has a clever response to just about anything. Israel is the tallest *vato* at HBI but somewhat slow on the uptake. "Mutt and Jeff" are also enemies and first-time flyers. As we are leaving for the airport, I notice that Israel is particularly excited about our trip. This is always nice to see—until, that is, we get in the car, and suddenly my Toyota Corolla smells like a brewery. I now know where Israel's bubbliness is coming from.

The Choir

The car ride is silent. I begin to worry that this will be a very long trip if these two rivals can't get beyond the artificial distance that's been set up for them. But a common terror of flying is always a reliable equalizer. On a small plane on a connecting flight to Knoxville, Israel goes into the restroom but can't figure out how to activate the light indicating that it's occupied. When the flight attendant notices and sees that lanky Israel has just entered, she announces over the PA system: "In order to turn on the light in the bathroom, you must bolt the door locked." He returns to his seat, red-faced. Soon the space between him and Gabino is bridged by a sharing of laughter and humiliation. Later, when Israel sees the pilot leave the cockpit to use the restroom (thinking he's the only one flying the plane), Gabino is the one to calm him down.

The next day, at the panel discussion at the Haley Farm, each man takes a turn at the microphones placed in front of him. Israel freezes up and his stories come out in an inarticulate jumble. Still, Gabino throws him a lifeline multiple times. He will not leave his "enemy" behind, drawing this "tall-ass" orphan into the fold of connection and inclusion.

The connection is solidified when we're on the plane home, about to land in LA. We are about ten minutes out, and the day is glorious and clear. Israel is by the window, Gabino is in the middle, and I'm on the aisle, all three of us straining for a view of the city.

"Hey, Israel, I can see your house down there," I say. I don't even know where he lives. He peers through the window with even more intensity. Gabino chimes in, the best possible Costello to my Abbott.

"There's your lady standing in front of your house." Israel looks even harder.

"Wait a minute," I add. "Who's that *vato* your lady's kissing in front of your house?" Gabino waves me off with a perfect volley, set, and spike over the net.

"Wait. I can read lips! She's saying, 'Hurry, hurry, Israel's plane is about to land!'" Gabino and I are giggly proud of our repartee. Israel finally peels himself away from the window and looks at us both.

"Wait," he asks Gabino. "You can read lips?" Consolation and invitation. We're brought in from the isolation and distance of having enemies and held close to the warm belonging God intends for us. "I won't leave you as orphans." Now go do the same.

A homie, daydreaming in my office, says, "Hey, G, let's go to Rome." I say sure, I'd love to. "Imagine, G," he says with a smile. "Pope Francis up in that balcony thing . . ." He stands and extends his arms, affecting something of a papal accent. "Homeboy Industries smells like sheep." I'm stunned that he knows this reference—Francis imploring his "shepherds" to get out of their offices so they can "smell like sheep." And there is no strain for the homie to grasp either smell or sheep. He knows that what's "original" in the program is the insurmountable concern for those on the edges, who have wandered or been excluded. He knows the smell of that.

There are two hundred references in Scripture that ask us to take special care of the poor. I'm guessing, then, it's important. It is this preferential care and love for the poor that sets the stage for the original program. It doesn't draw lines—it erases them. It rises above the polarizing temperature of our times. It doesn't shake its finger at anybody but instead helps us all put our finger on it. We could ask ourselves, I suppose, if God is conservative or liberal, but I think that's the wrong question. Instead we should ask: Is God expansive or tiny? Is God spacious or shallow? Is God inclusive or exclusive? What are the chances that God holds the same tiny point of view as I do? Well, zero. The Choir aims to challenge the politics of fear and the stances that limit our sense of God. It believes that a love-driven set of priorities will ignite our own goodness and reveal our innate nobility, which God so longs to show us. It invites us to inch the world closer to what God might have had in mind for it. And the poor are our trustworthy guides in this.

The original covenantal relationship in the Hebrew Bible (the *original* original program) went like this: "As I have loved you, so must you have a special, preferential, favored love for the widow, orphan, and stranger." God knows that these folks know what it's like to be cut off. And because they know this particular suffering, God finds them trustworthy to lead and guide the rest of us to the birth of a new inclusion, to the exquisite mutuality of kinship: God's dream come true.

When the gospel connects with our hearts and we find ourselves on the "outskirts," those on the margins may wonder what we're doing there. They aren't accustomed to our presence in their space. In the end, though, the measure of our compassion with what Martin Luther King calls "the last, the least, and the lost" lies less in our service of those on the margins, and more in our willingness to see ourselves in kinship with them. It speaks of a kinship so mutually rich that even the dividing line of service provider/service recipient is erased. We are sent to the margins NOT to make a difference but so that the folks on the margins will make *us* different.

Mike Kennedy, my superior years ago, would often ask his brother Jesuits, "Who are your friends? Are you friends with the poor?" Emily, a Homeboy receptionist for many years, grew up in the projects. With her kids, she uses a line her mom would use on her when she'd come traipsing home at all hours of the night: "Tell me who you're with and I'll tell ya what you're doin'." "See Jesus standing in the lowly place," Ignatius puts it. The lowly place is the locus of our true liberation. Walking with the poor, who are our friends, is mutually transforming and announces to the world something radically new. The poor, Jesus says, will enter this kinship before the rest of us, because that's what guides do. They go ahead of us. They get us there.

A homie, speaking to a city council meeting, addresses them

as if they were stand-ins for all of society. "You gave up on me even before you knew me," he says. So we are encouraged to stand with the tax collector and the prostitute, the widow, orphan, and stranger, precisely because they are the judged, the scapegoated, the less-than, whose chances are taken away well before they are given. The principal cause of suffering for the leper is not an annoying, smelly, itchy skin disease but rather having to live outside the camp. So the call is to stand with them, so that the margins get erased and they are welcomed back inside. Jesus doesn't think twice: he touches the lepers before he gets around to healing them.

When I worked in Cochabamba, Bolivia, after being ordained in 1984, I lived with Jesuits. My house job (by virtue of drawing the shortest straw) was to pick up the bread each morning. Now, in 1984, Bolivia was in the midst of an economic crisis, the poorest country in the western hemisphere. And bread was a staple. Beginning at 4:00 a.m., I'd *hacer cola* (stand in line) with the servants of the wealthy, awaiting our daily ration of loaves. I'd sit there on the sidewalk in the bitter Bolivian cold, covered in several blankets, leaning against an adobe wall for three hours like it was the Rose Parade or opening day of the latest *Star Wars* movie. When the bread would run out, every shop owner would turn his hand, like the wave of a queen to her subjects, to indicate that nothing was left.

One afternoon I was waiting for a bus. Sitting some feet from me on the sidewalk was an old beggar, blind and holding out a tattered hat, hoping someone would kick him down with a *limosna*. Traffic stopped at the signal, and a truck found itself directly in front of the blind man. It was an open-air truck, packed with exhausted campesinos covered in dirt. One of them, seeing the beggar, reached into his little rucksack and pulled out a golden loaf of Bolivian bread. Just like that, he dropped the whole thing—direct hit—right into the old man's hat. The beggar felt the impact, found the bread, held it up to his nose, and then hoisted it high, grateful to God and the donor, whom he now knew to be one and the same.

Dorothy Day simply asserted that "love and more love is the solution." And, true enough, love drives out all fear. The call to the margins, led by those we find there, is exhilarating and life-giving and renews our nobility and purpose. For this, we all long. The time is now, as never before, to put terror and defense to one side and find our human connection on the margins, where the original program is meant to take place. The Choir doesn't feel under siege or the need to "defend the faith." After all, our following of Jesus always has less to do with our words and more to do with our lives.

In the early 1990s, when I was pastor of Dolores Mission, the women in the projects devised a campaign to disarm their gang member sons and keep them safe. There'd be huge rallies in the playground of Pico Gardens, where the women would stand on a large platform with a big trash can and a microphone and implore other mothers to go into their children's bedrooms, lift up the mattresses, retrieve the Uzis, and throw them away. Some mothers actually did it at the rally, but most would more discreetly call me during the week. "*Oye, padre,*" they'd say. "I have some 'blankets'"—wink, wink—"to donate for the homeless men sleeping in the church." I'd go get them and, let's just say, they were really heavy blankets. The rallies became such an event in the neighborhood that even little kids would bring their toy guns for deposit.

Dianne Feinstein, during her failed gubernatorial run in 1990, heard of the rallies these ladies held and wanted in. Her people called me for permission to meet with the organizers, and though I assured her folks that I was but the "janitor" around here, I told them I'd deliver the message. I suppose I presumed that the women would be impressed with the invitation. "Dianne Feinstein wants to meet with *us?*" they would ask, with awe. There was none of that. They were clear and unanimous. They said in Spanish: "If she wants to come to listen to us, tell her to come. But if she's coming to tell us what to do, in our community, about gang violence, *dile que no venga* [tell her not to come]."

Feinstein never came, fearing, I think, that it might turn into the photo-op from hell. Widows showing the rest of us the way. Pope Francis writes that "the Gospel of the marginalized is where our credibility is at stake." The essence of our credibility lies not in our rescuing or saving the poor but rather by humbly surrendering to their leadership and listening to them. My spiritual director, Bill Cain, says, "Putting on Christ is the easy part, but never taking him off . . . that's a challenge."

I knew a kid, Carlos, who grew up in the projects, got into a gang, then got into some considerable trouble. Eventually he went to prison for a stretch and then was deported. Though he came to the United States from El Salvador, a two-year-old in his mother's arms, his homeland was a foreign country. I spoke better Spanish than he did. He was twenty-five and was forced to leave his entire family in Los Angeles, including his lady and their three-year-old daughter.

I get many calls from those who I name my "dearly deported"—homies who have been airlifted back to their birthplaces. They'll often reach out because they need money. Carlos was a regular caller. "Damn, G. Salvador's poor. It's a world country three."

"Uh, you mean a third world country?"

"Yeah, dat one."

Many, many months passed, and I hadn't heard from Carlos . . . until one day he called to tell me, to my surprise, that he was back in Los Angeles and needed to see me. I picked him up at his lady's in Pico Rivera. I had known him as a chubby kid, and that was the image I'd kept of him in my mind. The man in front of me now was gaunt and "sucked up," as the homies would say—but not from drugs, which was usually the reason for such an appearance.

The Choir

He had been on a most perilous odyssey and I heard all about it over a meal at Marie Callender's. His saga was months long, filled with harrowing starts and stops. He'd get so far in his trek home, then would get turned back by robbers or crooked authorities, nearly starving or freezing to death. There were also terrifying accounts of leaping out of moving trains and rolling down embankments, sometimes enduring great injury. If someone had filmed all this, you would look at the screen and say, *No way*. Incredible. He made it as far as somewhere in Mexico, where a gang of robbers didn't just relieve him of what little money and valuables he had but stripped him naked and left him alone. Somehow he managed to tiptoe his way into a tiny Mexican village, hands shielding his genitals, darting between and behind trees and then darting some more. His torso was covered in gang tattoos. When people began to notice him, he explained that he'd been robbed. Villager after villager began to hand him pieces of clothing. After some time, there he stood, in the middle of no-damn-where, fully clothed in other people's kindness. He was so overwhelmed by the fact that no one denied him or turned him away. "I made a promise, like a vow. I would be kind from now on because of these people's kindness to me."

And so he did, and it marked every interaction with any other human being as he made his way home. He encountered a young mother with a daughter, whom he adopted in his kindness vow, watching over them. He schooled them on riding the rails and hustled up food, often going without so that they could eat. He protected them from those who might want to cause them harm. One day, as they were riding on top of a train, they passed slowly through a town before picking up speed again. They spotted a small evangelical church with a *letrero* out in front. It was the kind of sign you'd see announcing the theme of Sunday's sermon.

The message in Spanish, unbelievably, said: "Carlos, I Am With You."

Carlos knew that it wasn't just a sign, but an actual *sign*—a confirmation of the purity of his vow and the truth of his goodness and promise. Tears streamed down his face as the train left the small town. The tenderness that was always and already there, found. The soft, unguarded place, capable of cherishing. He knew that he was going home, that it would happen. What goes around does come around.

I drove him home later that night, so moved by his account. I told him that his transition back to LA would be difficult but that I would help. In fact, I told him, "As I drop you off right now, I won't come to a complete stop, so you can jump out of my moving car." He howls.

"That will make me feel *so* at home."

Pope Francis states clearly, "Jesus wants to include." It's an odd way to phrase it, because it is a call to action in the present moment. Jesus' desire and longing and urge to include is happening *now*. It's about all of us wanting to stand where he stands and to include as he does. It is less about what it is we are to do at the margins, and more about what will happen to us if we stand there. Knowing homies has changed my life forever, altered the course of my days, reshaped my heart, and returned me to myself. They have indeed been trustworthy guides. Together, we have discovered that we all are diamonds covered in dust. They have taught me not that I am somebody but that I am everybody. And so are they. It's the original program.

Love and more love. It's what's left when the margins get erased. The Choir, living close to the gospel bone, finds itself anchored at the outskirts, putting on Christ and not taking him off. Choosing to be fearless for each other so we can find our true height in love.

Show of hands.

CHAPTER NINE

Exquisite Mutuality

I consider it a singular blessing in my life to have known Cesar Chavez. Though many celebrate his vision, his community organizing skills, and his ability to create and galvanize a movement, I most remember and admire his keen skill at listening. If you were speaking to him, he wasn't looking over your shoulder, eyeing a more important person on the approach. Nothing and no one else existed in that moment but you and whatever you were going on about. I wish I could pull this off. He embodied poet Judyth Hill's idea: "Wage peace with your listening."

I'm embarrassed to admit that, even when homies are lined up outside my office to see me, I am something of a multitasker. At my desk, I am the Rose Mary Woods of listeners—texting, opening letters, finishing a call, eyeballing who's next to see me, sending an email, and managing to erase eighteen minutes of the Watergate tapes. A very earnest sixteen-year-old gang member once stood in front of my desk and said, "Look. I need your divided attention." I said, "YOU . . . are in luck. Cuz that's EXACTLY what you'll be getting." Anyway, I wish I could listen like Cesar.

Once a reporter commented to Cesar: "Wow, these farm workers . . . they sure love you." And Cesar smiled, shrugged, and said, "The feeling's mutual."

When the feeling's mutual, we are seized by a tenderness that elevates us to the very largeness of God. As Christians, we want to bridge the gap that exists between people. Even in service, there is a distance: "Service provider . . . service recipient." Service is where we begin, yet it remains the hallway that leads to the ballroom. The ballroom is the place of exquisite mutuality. At Homeboy Industries, I'm not the "Great Healer" and that homeboy over there is in need of my precious healing. Truth be told, we are all in need of healing; we are all a cry for help. The affection of God unfolds when there is no daylight separating us.

No one has had more opportunities at gainful employment through Homeboy Industries than Droopy. Whether in our social enterprises or jobs we found for him in the private sector, he would always gravitate back to vague criminality, usually the sale or use of drugs. Then he'd invariably wander back to my office, asking for another chance. I had known him since he was a kid. He was exceedingly quick, with a dangerous sense of humor. Once, I was on the phone with him, trying to get a homie's phone number. There was a bad connection and, despite many attempts, I just couldn't make out the last four numbers. Finally, he paused in exasperation and bellowed "It's the year you were born! 18-63!"

Once, after a four-month stint in County Jail for a probation violation in his late twenties, he sat in front of me, ready to wipe clean his slate—again. He greeted me as he always did: "G-Biscuit! How you doin', you ol' goat?" (Ever since the movie *Seabiscuit*, he had taken to calling me "G-Biscuit.") I told him I was fine; the real question was how *he* was doing. "G," he said, leaning forward, "I'm new and improved." My face took me hostage and displayed some skepticism, but still I agreed to call a friend of mine named Gary who owns a vending machine company in Alhambra. As luck would have it, and as he had done before with other homies, he hired Droopy, sight unseen, telling me that he was happy to have him start the next day.

Gary is a holy man.

Two weeks later, Droopy was back in my office. *Híjole, madre santa*, I think. *Here we go again.* I waited for the excuses, the promise that it wouldn't happen again, that next time would be different. But he didn't say it. Instead, he retrieved something from his pocket: his very first paycheck from the vending machine company. He waved it wildly and pronounced, "Damn, G, this paycheck makes me feel proper. I mean, my *jefita* is proud of me and my *morritos* aren't ashamed of me." He pointed a finger at me and wagged it a little. "And you know who I have to thank for this job?" I reddened a little and my eyes struggled to meet his. I hemmed and hawed and aw-shucks'd so much you'd think I was from Mayberry. Finally, I smiled and asked who.

Droopy looked at me cockeyed, the way a dog looks toward a strange sound, and pointed skyward. "Well, God, of course." I fell over myself in agreement, as if I expected nothing less. He leveled his heat-seeking finger at me again. "You thought I was going to say you, didn't you?" I once again stumbled out of the gate. "No . . . gosh, no . . . I mean, of course . . . God's number one." Now *I'm* the one pointing upstairs. He finished me off. "You are so lucky we don't be livin' in dem Genesis days."

"I'm sorry," I said. " 'Dem Genesis days'?"

"Yeah . . . cuz God woulda BEEN HAD . . . struck yo ass down already by now."

In unison, we fell out of our chairs laughing, defying anyone to identify exactly who here is the "service provider" and who is the "service recipient." It's mutual.

I was once interviewed by PBS, and at the very end the guy asked me how it felt "to have saved thousands and thousands of lives." Not trying to be coy or cute, I told him I didn't know what he was talking about. I was not aware that I had saved any lives—I remain utterly convinced that my life has been saved, repeatedly, by the homies. When I need patience, the homies save me from my impatience. When I lack courage, they rescue me from my cowardice. And when I am completely convinced of the rightness of my position, the homies douse me with a big ol' bucket of humility. Days don't go by without them saving me. I told the interviewer that I thought "saving lives was for the Coast Guard."

An Aboriginal woman from Australia said to some earnest, well-intentioned missionaries: "If you're coming to help me, you are wasting your time. But if you have come because your liberation is bound up with mine, then let us work together."

A woman, quite determined to join our efforts at Homeboy, once told me she *had* to volunteer with us. When I asked her why, she replied, "Because I believe I have a message these young people need to hear."

"The minute you lose that message, come back to us," I replied. We don't point the cursor at some lost soul and push the "save" button. Many high school volunteers, long accustomed to building the orphanage or feeding the homeless in a soup kitchen, ask me what they're supposed to "do" at Homeboy, and I always answer: "Wrong question. The right one is: What will *happen* to you here?"

We always seem to be faced with this choice: to save the world or savor it. I want to propose that savoring is better, and that when we seek to "save" and "contribute" and "give back" and "rescue" folks and EVEN "make a difference," then it is all about you . . . and the world stays stuck. The homies are not waiting to be saved. They already are. The same is true for service providers and those in any ministry. The good news, of course, is that when we choose to "savor" the world, it gets saved. Don't set out to change the world. Set out to wonder how people are doing.

I met a man, an ex-homie, born-again and with the best of intentions, who was now working with gang members. "How do you reach them?"

"For starters, stop trying to reach them," I said. "Can YOU be reached by THEM?" Folks on the margins only ask us to receive them.

At Homeboy, we often say, "Community trumps gang." Only by offering a real, live community are you able to shine a light on the empty, shallow, and false "belonging" of a gang. Community is the singular place where patience and steadiness can be practiced, compassion can be expanded, and gratitude can be nurtured. There is a Navajo conception that a criminal is one who acts as if he has no family. This is in large part what we seek to supplant. Homeboy wants to provide a sanctuary for homies until they become the sanctuary they sought here. It is in that setting that we are able to calibrate our hearts and point them in the direction of the welcoming embrace. Here we make a decision to live in each other's hearts. After all, we are all just looking for a home for our hearts. As Dorothy Day writes, "We have all known the long loneliness and we have learned that the only solution is love and that love comes with community."

Emily is a homegirl who has become a member of our senior staff. She has a great deal of responsibility now, but she never forgets how she, too, once struggled with the same issues as our trainees. She's been there. On a Monday, she comes into my office to tell me about her weekend. "I sure was in a funk yesterday," she begins. She tells me she's been having trouble shaking the dark place that comes upon us all on occasion. "So I needed my Homeboy fix." She drove to our empty headquarters after dropping off her wife,

Amanda, at her part-time job, and circled the building several times in her car. "I felt better after that."

Later, she's driving home and stops at a red light at Cesar Chavez and Mission. She turns and sees that the car stopped in the next lane is me. She honks, and though I impulsively wave, I don't know who it is—the glare is too bright. Then I recognize her. We both roll down our windows, laugh, and go on about whatever. We're able, in that instant, to tell each other how much we love each other. Then the light turns green. Both of us depart, hearts elevated above the opaque thickness that surrounds us all sometimes. We both could touch, from our open windows, the fecundity of healing, the connection of community, and souls returned to their truth. All at a red light.

In Buddhism, a "sangha" is a community that lives in harmony and awareness. Our hope is that people are brought into harmony and a shared connected experience within our walls. We recognize our shared humanity. We find constant replenishing in ongoing mutual healing, because the truth is, Homeboy Industries is a trauma-informed community. The people find here a safety net and an ability to "regulate." We offer containment, safety. We hold them close, and everyone is given plenty of room.

Mutuality, like holiness, is irresistible. The shyest homie ever to enter our doors was a kid named Matthew. He lived in Boyle Heights and I had met him in a probation camp. He took my card there, and I waited to see if I'd get the call. I did, but the conversation was clearly painful for Matthew. He was so timid that it seemed like he might run out of self before it was over. He finished the call awkwardly: "I will get back to you when I can speak to you verbally." (I'm certain he kicked himself after he hung up.) I found out later, from a teacher at our alternative school, how terrified he was to actually speak with me in person. He asked the teacher, "But what if he uses big words . . . and I can't understand him?"

To his credit, he still showed up at my office at the designated time, despite his fears. I welcomed him aboard (keeping my words simple) and watched as he was handed off to an older homie, a navigator, who showed him around. In the weeks to come, I noticed him from my office, shyness melting as he was slowly shepherded by these large tattooed fellows who knew how to lead a timid soul to feel cherished and welcomed.

In the time since, Matthew took to entering my office and depositing his backpack against the wall of my domain for its protection. Lots of the part-timers do this. Usually he would drop it and run, with a perfunctory "Hello." One particular day, however, Matthew laid down his backpack, having just come from school, and sat in a chair in front of my desk. I was in the midst of reviewing a letter for a homie's court date and asked Matthew to wait a moment as I finished my proofreading. I felt bad that I was leaving him hanging, so I made some small talk to keep him engaged while he waited.

"So," I began, "how'd you get here today?"

"I walked," he said.

"Oh," I responded, returning to the final review of the letter awaiting my signature.

"Actually," he added quietly, "I came running."

I stopped reading and looked up at a kid who may never run out of self again. I smiled, and he did too. "That's right, *mijo*. That's right."

It would seem that God created an "otherness" so that we could find our way in mutuality to kinship. Margins manufactured by God, perhaps, so that we'd dedicate our lives to their erasure. We are charged not with obliterating our diversity and difference but instead with heightening our connection to each other. As it says in the Qur'an: "I create diverse tribes, so that you might come to know each other." And, to come running.

Many years ago, I gathered together in our conference room a group of hard-core gang interventionists who worked in different parts of Los Angeles. Every single one was a former gang member. Midway through the conversation, as expected, the "Step aside, let us handle this" moment occurred. In the early days, it happened a lot.

"Padre, with all due respect," someone would say, "I think gang members are more likely to listen to us than to listen to you." I would agree with them, but only if the task is primarily *talking* to them. Similarly, I'm often asked in the Q and A sessions that follow a talk—usually by a Chicano activist—about my alleged initial rejection from gang members because I am white. I always say that this was never an issue, though people always presume it will be. Fortunately for everyone, the solution has nothing to do with talking. Often enough we ask ourselves: How do we bridge the distance between "direct service" and "structural change"? I have learned that it's never about "saying" very much at all but, rather, receiving, listening, and valuing people until they come out with their hands up—feeling, for perhaps the first time, valuable. Receiving them and allowing yourself to be reached by them is all that's asked of us. And anyone who is the proud owner of a pulse can do this. Wage peace by listening.

One of the things that keeps us from the margins and the joy of mutuality we find there is our constant disqualifying of ourselves. "What could I possibly say to gang members?" "I've never been to prison; I don't have any tattoos." If it's about talking to gang members, then it is a rarefied, specialized effort. If it's about delivering that message that will save and alter that gang member's course, then it remains . . . about you saving the day. Listening and receiving is the great equalizer. Really. Who can't do that?

Alice, a longtime friend of mine, has asked to volunteer at Homeboy. I taught her sons at Loyola High School years before, and she was starting to slow down her real estate work in Hancock Park and wanted to teach art at our alternative school, Dolores Mission Alternative. It was a tough place filled with gang members. There were fights all the time, and stories of teachers' tenures lasting a minute and a half were numerous. Naturally, Alice doubted her ability to relate to the students, being a white woman from Hancock Park. Once a kid said to her, "Damn, Alice, you have one of them, you know, white-picket-fence lives!"

Still, she plodded on, always exceedingly kind and trying to make a connection to her charges through art. Each and every kid, Alice "received." One day she walked into the classroom to find that a homie had come in early. He was scribbling on a note-book—no doubt practicing his gang script and *placa*. He looked up, smiled, and said, "It's fuckin' Alice." Then he simply resumed his doodling. In that moment Alice knew she had arrived.

One year, at the Emmy Awards, many of our trainees were contracted out for the night to give directions and stand guard in the parking lot. They were dressed in black pants, crisp white shirts, and thin black ties, pointing celebrities to this place and that section. They were thrilled to do it. A big ol' homie named Rascal recalled his excitement the next day as we sat in my office. "I saw this short *vato* after the whole *pedo*," he said. "Damn, G, he had two Emmys! So I waved him over and said, 'Do me a *paro*? Hand me those.' So he did. I gave him my cell. And he took a flicka of me. Watcha." Rascal found the photo on his phone and held the screen in front of my face. There he was, beaming as he hoisted the two awards high above his head.

"Well, who was the short *vato*?" I ask him.

"I have no idea," Rascal replies, "but I took a picture, cuz I knew you'd ask."

The short guy was Martin Scorsese. Even in the aftermath of a gala awards show, we are all being asked to step away from our autonomous selves into the warmth of our alignment with each other. Both famous director and gang member had reason to joy-fully hoist their awards high.

Rene is having a bad day. He's at the bus stop, eating a peach and stuck in a funk he can't shake. It's a common experience for homies when as my friend Celeste Fremon says, they "realize how thrown away they are." Things get dark. Today the darkness is weighing more heavily on Rene than his usual list of burdens and woes. It is nearly paralyzing.

Every day, before he heads to work at Homeboy, he can be found at this bus bench. An elderly Japanese woman is also there every day. He doesn't know where she goes; maybe a senior center. She is bent over and appears to be too old to work. Everyone always makes sure she gets a seat on the bench. The bus arrives, and six or so folks around Rene begin to line up to board. Rene makes sure the Japanese *viejita* is ahead of him. As they make their way onto the bus, the old lady turns and says to Rene, "I admire you." This is the first time they've ever spoken.

"You do?" Rene asks. "Why?"

"You eat healthy," she says matter-of-factly. "Every morning you're here eating fruit. A banana. An apple. Today, a peach. You eat fruit. So I admire you." Rene helps her climb on the bus. They buy their tickets. She sits up front in the senior section. He sits in the back, in the unofficial "homie" section. He sits there and replays in his mind what the woman has said to him, and he realizes that the funk is gone.

He can't help himself. He works his way through the morning crush of commuting bodies and finds the Japanese woman. He gets on one knee and looks her in the eye. "Thank you for bringing so much spirit into my day." The woman smiles, she touches Rene's arm, and he returns to the back of the bus. Every moment, it turns out, is an invitation to recognize our interconnectedness. "You are the other me and I am the other you."

I was once trying to find a parking spot on the street near Homeboy and having a hard time of it. I usually avoid our parking lots—I want to reserve them for customers and clients—so now I was a full three blocks away, down some side street in a very in-dustrial area, when I came upon three members of our janitorial crew. We send them out to clean the streets in an effort to earn some neighborly goodwill with the local merchants. There were three of them: an African American gang member, a Latino gang member, and a white supremacist. We don't have too many of this last variety—a handful. But I'm heartened when these felons show up right out of prison, ready to begin their lives anew. All of our Caucasian trainees have been involved in white prison gangs. The three of them are working, talking, and laughing. Black, brown, white. The Kingdom of God at hand.

The scene reminded me of a time years ago when I drove up on our landscaping crew. The only difference was, they weren't working. They were all leaning on their rakes and shovels, shooting the bull. The Mexicans have an expression for folks like this, those who are particularly lazy: *huevón*. It literally means "large egg" but it casually refers to someone with enormous testicles—not in the "He has courage" sense but rather in the "Your testes are so large, you are having a hard time getting around" sense. So I see our "workers" resting on their tools, and I pull up alongside them, roll down my window, and pretend I don't know them.

"Excuse me," I call out. They lean in to listen. "I'm new around here. I'm trying to find where there is a Huevones Anonymous meeting nearby. I mean, I saw all of you leaning on your shovels, so I figured, '*They* must know where one is.'"

Omar, the "smart Alejandro" in the group, leans in. "Oh, are you our guest speaker today?"

The others laugh, high-five him, and lavish him with praise: "Good one." "Nice goin'." "I give ya credit."

How did I not see that one coming?

Now, as I watched these three new working men, I thought I would follow a variation on my old routine. I pulled up and rolled down the window on the passenger side. The three looked over and leaned in, their faces filling the window. Before they could yell "G!" in recognition, I asked: "I'm new around here. Can you tell me where I can find Homeboy Industries?"

The white gentleman is eager to be a full participant in the silliness. He leans in even more. "Yeah, well, you go down Main Street for three blocks. Make a right on Bruno. And there it is, Homeboy Industries. Right on the corner of Alameda and Bruno." He's giddy playing along. "Then you're gonna walk in there and you're gonna be greeted by a big, fat, jolly guy with a white beard."

My thought bubble reads, "What the what?" and my face may be suggesting the same. The other two workers are really laughing, but this fella's not so sure. His face says he's worried that he may have crossed a line. I seek to ease his concern. "I'm looking for Homeboy Industries, not the North Pole."

What Homeboy seeks is relational. Certainly silliness, among other things, can get you there. We do not care about imposing our advice or message or polishing up our winning argument. The novelist E. M. Forster repeats in a chapter of *Howards End*: "Only connect."

The rich young man asks Jesus, "How do I inherit eternal life?" This is not a question about heaven. We all want to get into heaven, but Jesus wants heaven to get into us. It's not about bank accounts or a tally sheet of good deeds. It's about the eternal life in connecting. Jesus shows us that before things become mutually beneficial at the margins, they need to be mutually relational. Only connect. Again, our separation is an illusion. God invites us to always live on the edge of eternity, at the corner of kinship and mutuality. We only seek to create a connection of hearts, to show others that they are seen, acknowledged, and embraced in the mutuality of value. We all just want someone to notice what we're eating, to take a photo of us with an award, to greet us with "It's fuckin' Alice."

I am invited to speak in Washington, DC, before a congressional select subcommittee on gangs. I bring some homies along. Louis and Joe are both very large gang members, in-need-of-seat-belt-extender kinds of fellows. En route to DC, we visit New York City, where Louis had lived until he was ten years old. As our plane is about to land, Louis asks Joe what's on his list of sites to see. "I wanna see the Statue of Liberty," Joe says, still peering out the window. "The Empire State Building, and, course, the Eiffel Tower."

Louis can't let this pass. "Fool, that's in Paris."

Joe does a smoldering turn to Louis and quietly says, "Well, then, I guess I'll scratch that off my list."

Once in DC, we speak before the committee and make the requisite stops to see our congresspeople in the hope that we'll get some slice of a funding pie. Afterward we have some time to get in some sightseeing. I decide to bring Louis and Joe to the Holocaust Museum. I had brought homies to the site many times before, and it's always a powerful experience for them.

The three of us begin in the lobby, where I tell them they'll have two hours to spend in the museum. "Let's walk the place alone—let it sink in—and meet back here at 3:00." Two hours later we are back where we started, debriefing. Clearly they were moved and even shaken by the weight of what they've just seen. While we're talking, we notice a man, probably in his eighties, sitting behind the desk, reading a book. He is tiny and bald and undistracted by our conversation. There is a chair placed in front of the desk that seems to invite someone to sit. Then we notice a small sign on the desk: "Holocaust Survivor." The three of us process this all at the same time and start to generate a response.

"What would we say to someone who has been through all that?" Joe asks quietly.

"Yeah," I add.

But Louis is fearless. "I'm gonna go talk to him," he says.

"You do that," I reply. "We'll be in the gift shop."

Louis later tells us about his encounter, with extraordinary and awestruck detail. The man's name was Jacob. He was thirteen when he arrived at Auschwitz. Both his parents were killed there. His two sisters were executed before his eyes, and a niece and nephew were also murdered. He was a worker and thus spared until the camp was liberated. Louis listened with all the attention that he could muster. When Jacob finished telling his story, Louis retrieved a Homeboy business card from his pocket. "I work at Homeboy Industries," he said. "It's the largest gang intervention, rehab, and reentry program in the world." Jacob took the card and studied it. "I hope," Louis added, "that if you're ever in Los Angeles, you'll come and visit us." Jacob remained quiet. "I'm twenty-seven years old," Louis continued, "and half those years I've been locked up."

Jacob, initially, feels moved to scoff. "In American prisons," he half chuckles, "you have your own room. A mattress. A pillow. We had to sleep on wooden planks. If you spoke in line, they'd pull you out and nearly beat you to death."

Louis takes this in, as if every word was some prized object being handed to him. "Yeah," he said, nodding with understanding. "I was beaten a gang a' times in County Jail. Once, I was pulled outta line and beaten so badly, I looked like the damn Elephant Man when they were done with me. And they threw me naked into a cell, where I slept on a metal sheet." Jacob now receives what Louis shares with a newfound reverence. It's at this point in his story, however, that I feel the need to intervene.

"Louis," I say, "let me see if I got this right. You were comparing your experience to a Holocaust survivor's?"

There is no hesitation for Louis. "No," he says with the clarity of a saint. "No, there is no comparing what this man has suffered and what I've lived through." Now he thinks and his eyes moisten before he speaks again. "No, I wasn't competing with him." A tear trails down his cheek. "I was connecting with him."

———

Part of the mutuality we foster and celebrate at Homeboy is born of the gratitude we feel for the history we share with one another. You can't force it, but you can watch it grow. I always tell the trainees to attempt this, despite the fact that homies associate the word "history" with the negative. A trainee will see a gang member sign in at the front desk, presumably seeking to redirect his life, and he'll point to him and say, "See that guy? We have history together." This is to say, it's not good. There's bad blood: he's an enemy or rival who has either caused mischief or been on the receiving end of it. But the hope is that homies will not just show up at our place, wash windows, and go home; bake bread and leave; serve tables, then call it a day. The hope is that we will lift each other out of our languishing isolation and rekindle a determination to show up. Instead of having a history, they will make a new one.

It's probably only been in the last five years or so that homies have started to ask me for my blessing. In the parking lot at Homeboy, before I enter the building, in the reception area, in my office—it can happen anytime, but most often it is requested on Fridays, before the weekend. The homies don't say, "Father, may I have your blessing?" Instead, they ask it in the exact same way.

"Hey, G—give me a bless, yeah?" This never varies.

I have an exasperating homie who works in the headquarters—though "work" may be too strong a verb. Robert is just eighteen years old, and no one complains and whines more than he does. There is always something wrong. Some supervisor is coming at him "sideways" or his check "came out short" or his case manager is giving him "the runaround" and does not help him "for nuuuuthing." I brace myself when he asks to meet with me, trying to locate my "best self" (I know you're in there; come out with your hands up) as the barrage of *quejas* begins. I ready my answer when he, the champion of all *pediches*, will also inevitably ask me to finish paying his electric bill or the last piece of his rent, which is always, coincidentally, due exactly that day; Robert has apparently mistaken this priest for an ATM. His financial situation is always dire: "I'm in the last critical stages," he'll say. "I'm in a strugglement prediction."

What's more, he never takes no for an answer. You can't derail him. He is persistent, unrelenting, and a USDA handful. Once I feigned a mystical experience in his presence. "Wait, wait," I said, holding him off with one hand. "I'm . . . I'm having . . . an out-of-money experience."

He didn't find it amusing.

Robert is one of the many orphans we have at Homeboy, a kid who raised himself, with no parents to speak of, who would rotate from couch to couch with other homies' families. It is downright astounding that he never bumped into the foster care system or landed on the desk of someone charged with noticing kids without families. Still, he's managed to rent a single apartment and is surviving. It makes his whining tolerable to know that he comes from such a place of abandonment and rejection, yet is able to live his own life productively. Though he has his moments of testing my patience, I always show him as much love and attention as I can. I try my best to listen. You give these kids more wiggle room.

Robert finishes his complaint-fest and desperate money-grab and finally ends our meeting with "Hey, G—give me a bless, yeah?"

He knows the drill. He approaches my side of the desk and inclines his head with all the devotion of a postulant. I place my hands on his shoulders. Suddenly, and fortuitously, I remember that the day before was his birthday. I haven't mentioned it yet, so I begin there.

"Robert, I am so grateful that you came into the world. Glad you were born. Yesterday was a holy day. I am a rich man because you are in my life. Never stop thanking God for making you as God did—He did a *firme* job. Even though"—and I'm not sure why I add this last part—"you can be a *huge* pain in the ass." Robert looks up with a beaming grin.

"The feeling's mutual."

Well, yeah. It is. Do we recognize a blessing when we see it? Once, while in the Dublin area for some talks, I was invited to visit

Saint Declan's, a school for kids with special needs. There were some forty students in the age range of six to twelve. Mainly boys, they were high-functioning autistic or Asperger's children, and all had emotional behavior issues. I arrived during the last hour of school and watched as, after a twelve-year-old threw a tantrum, the staff confined him to the "tantrum room," where he spit and flailed his limbs. I also sat in a classroom and witnessed an exceedingly patient teacher and his aides try to maintain order with eight young boys who were, let's just say, "unfocused." The phrase "herding cats" does not capture the task given to the adults in that room.

At the end of the school day, after all the students had been loaded onto their buses and were traveling safely home, I addressed the thirty-odd staff members still at the school. They were beaten and bruised, thrashed and spit upon. They were down but not out, wobbly but not defeated. It made me cry to see their faces. I told them how fortunate they were, because they showed up for work each day and their lives were saved because they did. Showing up at Saint Declan's each day rescued them from their self-absorption. It liberated them from their preciosity and cleverness. They were freed from meanness, petty obsessions, and ambition, and thrust themselves into this salvific maelstrom of spittle and swinging arms. Each face, the countenance of salvation.

After thirty years of doing this, I find myself endlessly grateful for the history I have with the people with whom I carry memories and routines and ways of speaking that cement our ongoing connection. It's not about giving and receiving; it's not about "It's better to give than receive"; it's not about "I received more than I gave." And it is not about "I just want to make a difference." It's mutual. This is why it can't be about you. If it is, then it becomes "collecting people," incessant ingratiating, and a frantic credentialing of self. What is hoped for is a lighter grasp, a gentler receiving. Can we love people, then have our reciprocal expectations disappear? I don't empower anyone at Homeboy Industries. But if one can love boundlessly, then folks on the margins become utterly convinced of their own goodness. We find our awakened connection to each other—a focused, balanced attention to the person in front of us. To reach and be reached, to savor the world, seeking only to receive the gift. And the world gets saved, and a decision gets made to live in each other's hearts.

An exquisite mutuality, lighting the whole sky.

CHAPTER TEN

Now Entering

O ver the years, I have learned countless things from the homies. In endless ways they have altered my heart and saved my life. But one of the most important and life-changing things they have taught me is how to text. I could not be more grateful for this lesson. Like all of us, I find it sure beats *actually* talking to people! I'm pretty good at it, if I do say so myself. I use LOL, OMG, and BTW like a pro, and the homies have even taught me a new one: OHN, which apparently means "Oh, hell no." I've been using that quite a bit lately.

The only thing that gives me trouble—and I know I'm not alone in this—is auto-correct. A homegirl named Bertha texts me on a Sunday: "Where you at?" I text her that I am about to speak to a roomful of "*monjas*" (nuns) and push Send. Auto-correct tells her I'm about to speak to a roomful of "ninjas." She thinks this is pretty interesting.

Another homie has his hair on fire about the money he needs to finish off paying his rent. I'd help him, but I'm short on funds at the moment, so I text, simply, "Things are tight." I push Send and auto-correct tells him: "Thongs are tight." He writes back. "Sorry to hear that," he says, "but, um, what about my rent?"

So I'm in a car with Manuel and Luis, on the way to speak to a gym filled with high school students. Manuel, as usual, has commandeered the shotgun seat and is close enough to me that I hear the sound of an incoming text message chime from his phone. He reads the text to himself and chuckles.

"What is it?" I ask.

"Oh, nothing. It's stupid. It's from Snoopy, back at the office." Snoopy and Manuel work in the clock-in room—clocking in hundreds and hundreds of workers. It's a tough job; I wouldn't want it. I had just seen Snoopy and given him a big *abrazo* before the three of us got in the car.

"Well, what'd he say?"

"Oh, it's dumb. Hang on a second." Manuel brings the message back to his screen. Then he reads: "Hey dog, it's me, Snoops. Yeah, they got my ass locked up at County Jail. They're charging me with being the ugliest *vato* in America. YOU have to come down right now. Show 'em they got the wrong guy."

I nearly drive into oncoming traffic, we're laughing so hard. Then I realize that Manuel and Snoopy are enemies, from rival gangs. They used to shoot bullets at each other. Now they shoot text messages. And there is a word for that: "kinship."

The kinship of God is where everyone matters. I visited a twenty-something homie named Duke in the hospital on December 25. He had been shot the day before, and I just found out. When I walked into his room, he asked with a smile, "So, what did you get me for Christmas?" The serrated edge of his usual attitude was not on display.

"Not a damn thing," I told him. "But it looks like God got you a proper-ass gift."

He surveyed me quizzically. "Yeah? What?"

"A second chance at life, *cabrón*."

"Oh, yeah. Dat." Duke adjusted himself to find comfort in the bed. "The doctor said that the bullet destroyed one fourth of my lung. That's almost half." I congratulated him on his mastery of fractions.

He quickly changed the subject. "Who you here to visit in the hospital?" he asked.

"What do you mean?"

"Who'd you come to see?"

"You, *menso*," I said, "who else?" Duke couldn't believe that he was the only reason for my presence at the hospital. He presumed I had a lengthy list of parishioners and friends to see. He must have thought that he would not make this list of those who matter. Folks on the margins find it hard to fathom that they, too, belong. So Duke's surprise at my visit was not all that surprising.

At a Congregational church where I've been invited to speak, the service begins with a unique translation of Revelations 21: "This is the story of the beautiful city of God. This city sparkles with the loveliness of rare gems. The city is filled with light. There are no shrines or temples because everything here is understood to be sacred and filled with the holy. This is the story of the beloved community. In this community we find welcome. In this community we find kinship. In this community we find our voice. In this community, all are loved." A homegirl said once, "When I arrived at Homeboy . . . it was like you all were waiting for me."

There is an African concept called *ubuntu* that describes a world without division. It makes nonsense of all that would separate us—color, religion, politics. It seeks only to heal and for-give. We seek the masterpiece of kinship in our union with each other. A homie once told me that, after his time with Homeboy, he no longer identified as a member of a gang but as a member of a team. We want to get to the edge, as Czeslaw Milosz says, where "there is no I nor Not I."

Demonizing and judging one another can't survive the plen-titude of community. With this beloved community, we cease to create a world that, unwittingly, makes life so tough on one an-other. What kinship always seeks to underscore is that separation is an illusion. However, we know that that doesn't just happen over-night. Rivals who work at Homeboy settle for solidarity before they arrive at kinship. One says to another: "I know we're not friends, but let's not be enemies." It's a good start, holding out for an even better ending.

Jesus was always inviting folks to move beyond the limitations of the blood family. The early Christians would greet one another with a kiss on the lips, which in those days only the members of the same family would do. Jesus has high hopes that we will move from separation to solidarity to kinship. God knows that we just keep waiting for the Kingdom to show up . . . just around the bend. Turns out, it *is* the bend. Just around the corner. The Kingdom is the corner . . . where we can kiss each other on the lips.

I'm walking to my car at the end of the day and I bump into Lorenzo. He's on his break from the bakery and is kicking it by himself by our lunch tables in the garden. After some small talk he says, "You know, my car just died on me this weekend. Middle a' no-damn-where, by myself. So, what do I do? Naturally—and you may not agree with this—I call my homies. First one says 'Hey, dawg, I'm in the middle of something. I can't go.' Next one, same thing. Over and over. 'I'm really busy dawg, sorry.' I called five of my homies and all said no. I didn't know what to do. So—I can't be-lieve this myself—I called Manny. We work together in the bakery.

I don't have to tell you, but there is no one in the bakery who is a greater enemy of mine than Manny and his 'barrio.' No one. But I had his number, so I called him." At this point Lorenzo slows the story down, as if he's hearing it for the first time. "And you know what my worst enemy said to me when I called him?" His eyes are suddenly and surprisingly moist. "He said, 'On my way.'"

Bugsy and Miguel were homies both sentenced to rehab. It would be difficult to identify two gang members who hated each other more. They never worked at Homeboy, but I knew them both from the streets. They belonged to rival gangs, though their hatred of one another was personal and not just due to card-carrying animosity. I would visit them on Sundays and initially was instructed to see them one-on-one, since they couldn't stomach speaking with me together. During his stay, Miguel wrote me asking for money for "cosmetics" (hygiene or personal effects), which I happily sent along. When I made my Sunday visit some weeks later, Bugsy and Miguel insisted on a shared meeting.

"You know the forty bucks you sent me?" Miguel asked. "I gave Bugsy twenty." Miguel waits a beat, for all the pieces to fall into place. "I guess," Miguel continued, "all I needed to do was meet his insides." Demonizing will always wither under the heat of kinship. It melts at the sight of our shared belonging.

Another homie, Marcos, and I are checking in as the day begins at Homeboy. The office door is open and in walks Giovanni. No one takes much notice anymore that the two men were once serious rivals who used to shoot at each other. They shake hands like any other day. "I'm going to the bakery," Giovanni says. "You guys want something? You know, like a cup of coffee, a corsage, or something?" Marcos and I eye each other and mouth the word "corsage" in the same instant. Giovanni makes a small baked-good gesture. "You know, a corsage. What do they call 'em."

"A croissant?" I ask.

"Yeah, you want one of those?"

I indicate no, but Marcos says that he'll have one. Giovanni makes for the door. Marcos quickly shouts after him. "But I'm *not* going to the prom with you!"

Now, we can be astonished at the authority of Jesus, who calls us to love our enemies. Or we can just love our enemies and so astonish the world as to jostle it from its regular course.

We're about to leave a fancy outdoor fund-raiser when we realize we're missing someone from the van. It's Vickie, a very tough homegirl, a shot-caller in her neighborhood and not someone to mess with. I ask another homie, Joel, where she is. Joel is a tall, goofy, awkward guy. He points to the dessert table, which is covered with, let me just say, the most amazing array of cakes and pies and every imaginable delight. Joel and Janet are from enemy gangs, a river filled with bad blood between them. "Go get her," I tell him. "Tell her we're leaving." But instead of walking over to her, Joel cups his hands around his mouth and, like the public address system of a squad car, shouts: "Vickie! Step away from the cheesecake!" *This is it,* I think to myself in horror as all the guests turn and look. War declared. But instead Vickie doubles over with laughter, and so does Joel. They walk into each other's arms. A step beyond solidarity; that much closer to the entrance marked "Kinship of God."

When Jim Carrey visited, hoping to establish a series of meditation trainings for our homies, a small group of us had lunch in the Homegirl Café. There were five of us at the table, and Carrey was trying to make a point about the illusory nature of separation. "Take this knife," he said, grabbing a knife from his set of silverware and holding it high by the handle. "And see my hand here?" His left hand was held out before him on the table. "Let's just say . . . that I stabbed my hand with it." His right hand, with the knife, came down hard. His voice and face were, well, a mix of Ace Ventura and Hannibal Lecter. The knife was positioned between his fingers. We all had the same reaction, which Carrey pointed out. "See? Each one of you grabbed your own hand and said 'Shit,' thoroughly connected to me." His tone shifted as he gently laid the knife down. "So, separation is an illusion."

For Jesus, the self that needs to die is the one that wants to be separate. This is the self that recoils from kinship with others and balks at union at every turn. It is the self that wants it all to remain private and thinks it prefers isolation to connection. We know that the early Christians believed that "one Christian is no Christian." This larger sense of belonging to each other acknowledges that many are the things that connect us, and those things that divide are few and no match for our kinship.

———————

We think that Jesus wants a fan club. Undulating crowds, gushing adorers, clamoring for autographs and sidling up to him, proclaiming, "I'm your biggest fan. I have all your albums. I've never missed a concert!" As is often said, Jesus does not say in the gospel, "Worship me," but simply "Follow me."

I recall being interviewed on the Christian Broadcasting Network by a woman who, having just listened to my litany of things we do at Homeboy Industries, from tattoo removal to job training, case management to mental health counseling, paused cautiously once I had finished. "But how much time do you spend at Homeboy Industries each day, you know, praising God?" she asked.

I actually didn't know what to say to that, but found myself offering: "All damn day."

How does praise please God, anyway? Or what would God find pleasure in? Find the thing that quenches God's thirst. Since God is on the receiving end of all this praise-filled attention, it would seem to make sense to ask ourselves: What kind of praise does God have any interest in? Does exaltation matter to our "exhausted" God?

I received an award once at a gala dinner. I was the second to be recognized, and the woman before me was breathless and seemed hugely panicked while giving her acceptance speech. "First, I have to thank Jesus Christ," she began, "because, after all, without him I am nothing." And all I'm thinking is: hostage video. I'm imagining Jesus offstage, behind the curtain, holding this woman's dog with a pistol to ol' Fido's temple.

"That's right," Jesus says, and nods. "Damn right, ya better thank me."

I already knew that in my speech I wouldn't be thanking Jesus. This is not because he is less important to me or my life. But I know, with all the certainty of my being, that Jesus has no interest in my doing this. To just say, "Jesus, Jesus, Jesus, I'm your biggest fan," causes him to stare at his watch, tap his feet, and order a double Glenlivet on the rocks with a twist. Fandom is of no interest to Jesus. What matters to him is the authentic following of a disciple. We all settle for saying, "Jesus," but Jesus wants us to be in the world who he is.

If you read the Acts of the Apostles, it doesn't say that people "prayed in tongues" but were suddenly able to hear those around them speaking "in their own native language." It is, as Marcus Borg points out, "the reversal of Babel," when languages get confused and division, rivalries, and misunderstanding become commonplace: it's the polar opposite of kinship, but it's also the beginning of something: an amazing possibility of reunification. Somehow the highest praise of God is not in speaking unintelligibly but, rather, in speaking a language of inclusion where barriers are dismantled, circles are widened, and no one is left outside. No one. People hear their language spoken and feel brought in and welcomed as never before. Safe to say, *this* pleases God, because it is God's only passion.

It would seem important to test what kind of praise is the right kind—the kind that just might bring a smile to God's face. We think the praise required of us is the maintenance of a constant state of astonishment at Jesus. Personally, I don't think he wants so much for us to wave palm fronds at his authority, but rather to locate our own—to be not so astonished at Jesus's authority but to live astonishingly, inhabiting our own power to live as he would.

We have an annual five-day retreat for all the trainees at Homeboy—one for men and one for women. Needless to say, God is exceedingly pleased by the bond between homies that becomes evident at the trip's end. When one group returned to the office, I asked Anthony, a six-foot-three-inch African American gang member, and Chino, a five-foot Vietnamese gang member, how they fared on the retreat. Anthony placed his arm around Chino's shoulder and smiled. "I haven't wanted to strangle him once," he proclaimed.

God is pleased.

———————

Our quest for kinship is fueled by the engine of hope. As the great Shirley Torres, director of reentry services for Homeboy Industries, told our staff during our financial crisis: "If we lose hope, there's no hope to give them." Through hope, we gain the unshakable belief that our lives are workable. It is only together that we can realize our hearts are resilient things, able to hold inexhaustible freedom and compassion.

Horacio, a young homie at a Youth Authority facility, is about to be released and is frightened. He's been close to leaving before, but then he gets into a fight or starts a brawl that derails his plans. He did this once during a mass of mine there. Communion time arrived, and suddenly he was flying through the air, *Matrix*-like, pummeling every enemy in line to receive communion. The supervising staff took out their pepper spray, covering us all in a cloud of gas. It is the only time I've ever been pepper-sprayed. We were all down on the ground, trying to stay below the fumes, when I turned to the homie next to me and asked if he thought mass was over.

"Trust me," he says, chuckling. "Mass is over."

I took a leave from mass duties at the facility while going through chemo, and when I returned, the guys presented me with a shadow box containing a photo of the homies—and the spent pepper spray canister. It is a cherished possession of mine. Horacio also stood up and publicly apologized for starting the riot that had taken place months before. Then he asked to speak with me. He was terrified of leaving the only place he'd known as home.

"What are you afraid of?" I asked him when we were alone.

After a long silence, he looked at me. "I'm afraid I'll forget my hope."

"Hope does not disappoint," Saint Paul tells us. This is always a challenge with gang members—who, more often than not, don't think their own death is a waste but think that their lives are.

"I'm messin' up in school," a young homie tells me. When I ask him why, he says without hesitation: "I know why. I don't have a dream. Ya gotta have a dream, something to look forward to." Hope is not about some assurance that everything will work out but rather about a confidence that purpose and luminous meaning can be found there, no matter how things unfold. "The self-fulfilling prophecy of the nihilistic threat," Cornel West writes, "is that without hope there can be no future, that without meaning, there can be no struggle."

At Homeboy, there is no such thing as "false hope." It is never about how many people we help. It's only about the hope we give, and hold out for them. None of it is wasted, or untrue. I once bumped into a kid I knew at Juvenile Hall. I spotted him at mass and went to go see him in his unit afterward.

"What they get ya for?" I asked.

"Reckless driving. But I don't remember."

I got out my pen and a piece of paper so I could look up his court date and such when I returned to the office.

"What are you under?"

"Medication."

"No, son. Your name."

He told me, and we finished up our conversation. Before I

left, he said to me: "You know what my problem is, G? I don't got no destination."

Another homie tells me, "I'm always thinking ahead, but only one step ahead." He adds, with a tint of sadness, "I'm so distant from the hope of myself." This kid isn't longing for advice. Hope is in the relationship, in seeing Jesus and being Jesus.

A woman once scheduled an appointment with me, and before I knew it she was unleashing the myriad ways God was disappointed in me and Homeboy Industries.

"As a Bride of Christ, I need to tell you that this place does not give glory to God," she said. I listened until I no longer could.

"Look," I said kindly, "thanks for visiting and bringing me this important message. But you see all those people out there?" I pointed to the reception area packed with gang members waiting to see me. "I only have an hour left to see them all."

She stood huffily. "So you're telling me these people are more important than the Lord?"

"No," I said as I walked her to the door. "Jesus thinks they *are* the Lord."

I was hungry, and you gave me to eat. I was thirsty, and you gave me to drink. I was a gang member without hope, and you gave me some.

A lifer at Lancaster prison told me once that he'd discovered compassion breeds hope. That's exactly what we aim to do at Homeboy. Every day we try to create an environment where an optimal healing process can take place—an environment where one can truly be helped through the process, and thrive. A community so loving that everyone feels like they're wearing a parachute.

It was well over twenty years ago that two fifteen-year-old gang members were sitting on a cement ledge in the darkness of Aliso Village Housing Project. I was riding my bike through the project—patrolling, I guess. These were the violent years, the decade of death between 1988 and 1998. There were shootings day and night.

These two boys, Edward and Robert, were, I suppose, talking about girls, *chismeando* about the barrio, regaling each other on exploits in school and beyond. Perhaps they were actually planning their futures rather than their funerals, unlike so many of their peers. Then I showed up, straddling my beach cruiser, giving each the "homie" handshake. Robert, who would die some years later in a car accident, was articulate and dominant. Edward, who would become a published poet, possessed that kind of soul, even if he hadn't yet discovered the craft. Both were *cariñosos* in their way, but Edward more so, ebullient and funny and right out there. Nothing got in the way of his love for you. To be in their presence was like taking an elixir: you always felt favorable. I don't know how they pulled this off, but they always did.

One of them—I can't remember which—suddenly blurted out, "Damn, G. Why can't you be our father?"

This was so easy to answer. "*Serio pedo*, on everything I love, if you two were my sons, I would have thought I had won the whole damn *lotería*. I'd be the proudest man alive and so grateful to God."

There was silence until one of them pointed frantically toward the darkness of the parking lot and gasped, "What's that?"

I turned, ready for armed "enemies" creeping in on a "mission." This happened a lot in those days. Sometimes marauding gang members would see me and they'd turn back. Other times they didn't know I was there and would open fire. But I saw no movement and the silence remained undisturbed. I turned back to the two boys and quickly realized their diversion tactic. They were both holding their faces in their hands, crying. They found their hope and "destination" in relationship, love as the only reliable salve there is.

Lately, protests suggest that without justice there can be no peace. Others might soften that message by saying, "If you want peace, work for justice." And this is true. But I think it is even more true to say: "No kinship, no peace. No kinship, no justice. No kinship, no equality."

In the bad old days, I once witnessed two cops "hem up" three tiny homies at the corner of Third and Gless. I was getting ready for mass, opening the windows to air out the church, when I saw our homies with their arms over their heads, like travelers walking through the TSA machines at the airport. The cops patted them down but found no drugs or guns. This apparently annoyed one of the police officers enough that he took a huge wad of gum out of his mouth and rubbed it in the hair of the tiniest *vato* there, a kid named Beto. Then the cop grabbed Beto's cap from the sidewalk and placed it back on his head, holding it down for a few counts so the gum would stick, before sending the three boys on their way.

The next day I met with the captain at the Hollenbeck police station to relay what I'd seen the day before. When I asked him what he thought the officer's goal was in treating the kids this way, he didn't need much time to formulate a response. "Father," he said, "the strategy is a simple one: make life as miserable as we possibly can for the gang member." I had to be the one to break it to him that life is *already* miserable for the gang member.

Cut to some years later, when a homie named Arnold stopped me in the projects. "Hey, G, you know an Officer Gomez?" he asked. I said no and braced myself for a horror story so common in the bad old days. But Arnold smiled broadly instead. "He's *firme*." He told me that the night before, as he walked Fifth Street—the area where crack was notoriously bought and sold—he was stopped by an Officer Gomez.

"What are you doing out here?" he asked. Arnold remained silent. "Look," Gomez continued. "I just wanted to say congratulations. I hear you're a brand-new, first-time father. *Felicidades.*"

Arnold was startled that this cop had such personal information about him. "Were you there when the baby was born?"

"Yeah," Arnold said, warming up. "I was there when my son popped out. It was amazing. I had to leave a couple of times, you know, to throw up. But I was mainly there."

"Good for you, *mijo*," Gomez said, patting him on the back. "I was there when all my kids were born too. Now, look, where you're standing right now is pretty dangerous. You know guys shoot from that freeway." Gomez pointed just beyond where they stood. "If I catch you slanging crack, I'll have to pop you. And you can't be a father to your son if you're in prison—or worse: dead. So go home. You'll be a great father. And your son needs one."

The Buddhists work with conflict by dropping the struggle altogether. This was what Officer Gomez did as he pivoted to a certain curiosity. Defensiveness was unnecessary. Neither were "bad guys," and they empowered each other to lean past the labels they previously had for the other. "Mercy," Mary Oliver says, "is when you take people seriously." Both men did this.

It is true enough that we could make the world more just, equal, and peaceful, but something holds us back, in all our complicated fear and human hesitation. It's sometimes just plain hard to locate the will to be in kinship even though, at the same time, it's our deepest longing. So no matter how singularly focused we may be on our worthy goals of peace, justice, and equality, they actually can't happen without an undergirding sense that we belong to each other. Seek first the kinship of God, then watch what happens.

It sometimes will occur to colleges and universities to force their students to read *Tattoos on the Heart* against their will and then invite me to speak on campus. The entire freshman class at my alma mater, Gonzaga University in Spokane, Washington, was strong-armed into reading my book. And I couldn't be more grateful. So, at their invitation, I brought two homies to join me for the trip. When hosts are willing to foot the bill, I always search out homies or homegirls who have never been on a plane before to accompany me. This time I took Bobby, an African American gang member who worked in the bakery, and Mario, who worked in our retail store.

We flew from Burbank Airport, which is a small and intimate experience. The planes are in full view from huge bay windows. There are no hermetically sealed chutes you must walk through to board: passengers walk on the tarmac and climb the stairs located at the front and back of the plane. I've probably traveled with hundreds of gang members over the years, but no one has ever been as terrified of the experience as Mario was. He was hyperventilating, gasping and flushed—and we hadn't even approached the aircraft yet. Our plane arrived, and as folks disembarked, I pointed it out to Mario, who was all but holding his head between his knees. Then I saw two female flight attendants climbing up the front stairs of the plane, each carrying two Venti-size drinks from Starbucks.

Mario emerged long enough from his terror tunnel to ask with a panicky whine, "When are we gonna board the plane?"

I pointed to the coffee-trudging flight attendants. "Well, as soon as they sober up the pilots." I know. I probably shouldn't have said this.

I should mention that Mario, a tall drink of water, is among the most tattooed of any of our trainees—and at Homeboy Industries that's saying a lot. His arms are "sleeved out," neck blackened with the name of his barrio, and his entire face is covered but for the immediate area around his eyes, nose, and mouth. I had never been in public with him and was surprised by people's reactions in the Burbank airport. People would widely sidestep him. Mothers would pull their kids in more tightly. The recoiling was pronounced and widespread.

And yet, were you to ask anyone at Homeboy who is the kindest, gentlest person who works at Homeboy, they wouldn't say me. The answer would most certainly be Mario. He is proof that only the soul that ventilates the world with tenderness has any chance of changing the world.

As always happens, I'm usually invited to give some evening keynote. What they neglect to tell you is that they have lined up many side events during our stay. Multiple classes, meetings with campus groups, etc. I told Mario and Bobby that they would speak at these things while I sat in the back of the room. Even though they both were quite nervous speakers, their accounts always moved people deeply. Their stories were filled with violence, abandonment, torture, and abuse of every kind. Honest to God, if their stories had been flames, you'd have to keep your distance, otherwise you'd get scorched.

So I changed things up at the evening keynote. I asked them to get up before me and each do a five-minute presentation in front of a thousand people so that I could include them in the subsequent question-and-answer session. Both were nervous, especially Mario, but they expertly delivered an edited version of the life stories they had presented earlier in different classrooms. I gave my usual speech, then invited the two homies to join me at the podium.

Once the room settled, I encouraged the audience to just raise their hands and belt out their questions without the aid of a microphone. The first question was from a woman near the front. She stood and said that she had a question for Mario. The spine shiver that went through his slim body was likely visible from any seat. He gingerly approached the mike.

"Yes?" he squeaked.

"You say you're a father," the woman began, "and your son and daughter are starting to reach their teenage years. What wisdom do you impart to them?" She recalibrates. "I mean, what advice do you give them?"

She sat, and Mario was left alone to sift her words and find a response. He trembled some, and closed his eyes, then suddenly blurted out: "I just..." As soon as those two words left his mouth, he retreated again to silence. Standing next to him, I could feel, sense, and see the sentence he was putting together in his mind, reducing him to a new, emotional setting. His eyes were closed and he was clutching the microphone. He finally opened his eyes and stretched his arm out toward the woman as if he were pleading with her. "I just... I just don't want my kids to turn out to be like me." His last words felt squeezed out and his sobbing became more pronounced.

The audience was silent, and not one of us made a move to fill it. The woman stood up again. Now it was her turn to cry as she pointed at Mario, her voice steely and certain, even through her tears. "Why wouldn't you want your kids to turn out to be like you?" she said. "You are gentle, you are kind, you are loving, you are wise." She steadied herself, planted herself firmly. "I *hope* your kids turn out to be like you." There was not much of a pause before all one thousand attendees stood and began to clap. The ovation seemed to have no end. All Mario could do was hold his face in his hands, overwhelmed with emotion.

Bobby and I each lightly placed a hand on his back as he gently sobbed and a roomful of strangers returned him to himself. As I looked at this crowd, it was unshakably clear that they, too, had been returned to themselves. It was all exquisitely mutual. An "orphan" guiding us to the birth of a new inclusion. A lanky tattooed gang member befriending his own wound and inoculating this room from despising the wounded. Everyone recognizing themselves in the brokenness. All of us, a cry for help, judgment nowhere in sight. And, yes, entering, just right now, into the fullness of kinship.

And I think that's the only praise God has any interest in.

"If we walk in the light," the apostle John writes, "then we have fellowship with each other . . ."

All of us kin and kissing on the lips.

To lose the earth you know, for greater knowing; to lose the life you have, for greater life; to leave the friends you loved, for greater loving; to find a land more kind than home, more large than earth—

Seek first the kinship, and watch what happens.

EPILOGUE

What Martin Luther King Jr. says of church, could well be said of this book: "It's not the place you come to, it's the place you go from." And the hope is that one goes from this humble effort of a book to the margins and the nurturing of the kinship of God. Homeboy Industries has always been the "already and not yet." What this place announces to the world is aspirational and not declarative of a fully formed, complete thing. Our community has always been about longing; always the desire for the desire.

Recently I was invited to speak to a group in West Covina called Men of Faith. The room was packed at the upper hall in the Knights of Columbus building. Bingo was happening below us. Men who longed for something larger gathered to be fed by our spacious God through each other. I was humbled to stand before them and was edified by their earnest yearning. I spotted Danny in the audience. He had taken a bus from downtown after work at the Homeboy Diner, the only place you can get food in LA's City Hall. Twenty-two years old, Danny was a handful in his day. After nearly ten years locked up, in and out, he had now settled into some abiding comfort in being his own truth and inhabiting his own goodness. I give him a ride back to Union Station after the talk.

I ask him about work and how business is going. He tells me, "I never saw myself as a "customer service" guy . . . but now I am one." I have him run down the menu for me, and when he gets to the sandwiches, he says, "We handcraft them." This seems like a charmingly odd verb for a former gang member to use.

As he fills me in on his life and lady and daughter and such, he says, "I'm happy with myself, G." I tell him that he has every reason to be proud. "Huh," he says, "that is not a word I would use. Proud." He weighs it all for a second and then says, "Thanks."

I pull up to the front of Union Station, where Danny will take a train to his home in the San Fernando Valley. "I wish I could give you some *feria*, dog," I tell him," but I've been in the office all day at Homeboy . . . and hit up by homies. I have no money at all."

"I'm good, G," he says. "Don't even trip. Got enough to take the train, with five bucks extra . . . so I can hand it to someone right now who needs it more than me." He opens the door and puts one foot out and takes a deep breath. "I got air in my lungs," turning to me, "I'm good. Love you, G."

We all go from here to breathe deeply the spirit of the One who delights in us and is always astounded at our thrilling discovery of our own goodness and light. We hope against hope to be reached by those on the edges of our circle, who give their last five dollars away, recognizing a need greater than their own.

This is indeed the place we go from.

ACKNOWLEDGMENTS

It is, indeed, the "grateful heart that transforms the world," so to that end I want to re-dedicate myself to thankfulness. I would refer the reader to the five pages of "*gracias*" at the end of *Tattoos on the Heart*. Glancing over those names now of family, friends, Jesuit brothers, and coworkers, I'm struck by their steadfastness still. My love for them knows no bounds.

Again, I want to thank my agent, David McCormick, and all his good staff. Jonathan Karp, the publisher at Simon & Schuster. The great Jofie Ferrari-Adler and the team there: Julianna Haubner, Stephen Bedford, Lisa Rivlin, Kathryn Higuchi, and Erin Reback Cipiti (I'll see you at Santa Anita's opening day!).

Just four other folks to thank:

Sergio Basterrechea, my spiritual director, who has taught me how to find God "resting in me and me, resting in God."

Tom Boland, indefatigable, faithful, and ever vigilant Assistant and friend.

Acknowledgments

Tom Vozzo, CEO of Homeboy Industries. I do not know where we'd be without you. Thanks for your leadership, tenacious spirit, and kind heart.

And finally, to Mary "Sol" Rakow, who gently guided this book so that it would be more kind and more resemble God's tender glance. You've guided my heart, as much as this book.

ABOUT THE AUTHOR

Gregory Boyle was ordained a Jesuit priest in 1984. He earned his Master of Divinity from the Weston School of Theology and a Sacred Theology master's degree from the Jesuit School of Theology. In 1988, Boyle began what would become Homeboy Industries, now located in downtown Los Angeles. He's received the California Peace Prize, the Humanitarian of the Year Award from *Bon Appétit*, the 2008 Civic Medal of Honor from the Los Angeles Chamber of Commerce, and was inducted into the California Hall of Fame. He is also the author of *Tattoos on the Heart*.

The author is donating all of his net proceeds from this book to Homeboy Industries. Visit the author at HomeboyIndustries.org.